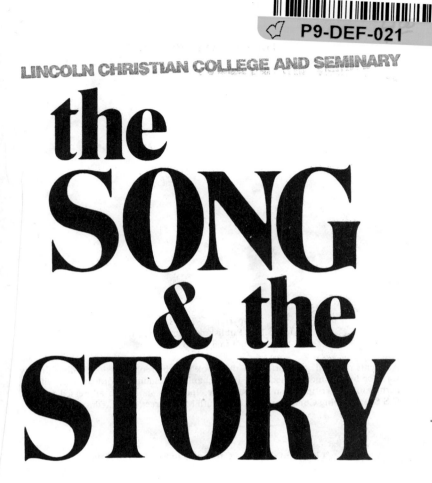

the SONG & the STORY

GEORGE M. BASS

Lima, Ohio
C.S.S. Publishing Company

THE SONG AND THE STORY

Copyright © 1984 by
The C.S.S. Publishing Company, Inc.
Lima, Ohio

Library of Congress Cataloging in Publication Data

Bass, George M., 1920-
  The song and the story.

  Includes bibliographical references.
  1. Preaching. 2. Public worship. I. Title
BV4211.2.B27 1984   251   83-73126
ISBN 0-89536-652-5

Library of Congress Catalog Card Number: 83-73126

1970/ISBN 0-89536-652-5   PRINTED IN U.S.A.

For all of my students at Northwestern Lutheran Theological Seminary and Luther Northwestern Theological Seminary — with appreciation and gratitude.

Table of Contents

Introduction

The past one and a half decades have witnessed a concerted effort to improve the worship and the preaching of the church, the Song of the people of God gathered together to offer thanks and praise for his blessings, and the Story — the gospel — told in one form or another by the preachers in their sermons. This liturgical-homiletical renewal is ecumenical in dimension, all-inclusive in its scope, and theological in its roots. It has the character of a "new Reformation," to use Bishop John Robinson's term, but it goes beyond anything he envisions in his book by the same title, or in his *Liturgy Coming to Life.* From one perspective, this renewal seems to be an extension of the liturgical-homiletical reforms instituted by Martin Luther in the sixteenth century; "The Constitution of the Sacred Liturgy" that was produced by Vatican II appears, at places, to have been lifted from the writings of Luther. *Word and Table,* published by the United Methodist Church in the United States as a guidebook for worship and preaching, springs from the same roots and demonstrates how widely the movement has spread. The renewal is real and it affects most of the Christian churches one way or another; its roots really go behind the Reformation to the shape of worship in the early church.

Among Protestants, the sermon has been the object of the most intensive attempt to improve one dimension of worship, the proclamation of the Word. The quality of preaching has become an ecumenical problem, but Protestants have long been aware of the "preaching dilemma" which Clyde Reid described in *The Empty Pulpit* in 1967, and homiletical literature reveals the extent of the efforts expended to improve preaching in the churches. Even in liturgically-oriented denominations, little attention was paid to the liturgy, the setting in which the preaching occurred, probably because most Protestants consider Sunday worship basically to be a preaching service. Bolster the preaching of the pastors, the literature seems to say, and worship in the form of the "Protestant Preaching Service" will be overhauled.

The form of the sermon was part of the problem, just as communication skills were connected to the weaknesses of the pulpit. Some of the first efforts toward renewing preaching came in the area of communication (as in Reuel Howe's *The Miracle of Dialogue* and *Partners in Preaching*), which led to attempts to alter monological sermon shapes into dialogical sermon forms — again, with little concern for worship. With few exceptions, all of the books on preaching that have appeared since 1967 (Reid's *The Empty Pulpit,* Howe's *Partners in Preaching,* and my *Renewal of Liturgical Preaching* were all published on the same day that year) have concentrated on developing the form of the pulpit message (exceptions include David Babin's *Week In, Week Out: Another Look at Liturgical Preaching,* Paul Bosch's *The Sermon as Part of the Liturgy* in Concordia's Preachers Workshop Series, and William Skudlarek's *The Word in Worship*). Some of the homiletical prescriptions stressed improving the content of the sermon, as well as, or rather than, the form of the homily itself. (*Proclamation,* the Fortress Press series of exegetical helps, does little for sermon shape in its homiletical "helps"; Richard Lischer concentrates on content in his *A Theology of Preaching*, but, in fairness to him, he touches on other problems.) There has been some discussion of preaching within the Eucharist, but not much on what the restoration of the Eucharist as the chief service on Sunday might mean for preaching and the sermon. (Fred Lindemann addressed this problem and the function of the sermon as part of the liturgy in 1958 in *The Sermon and the Propers.*) Evidence shows that, even though it is a slow process, Holy Communion is becoming the main order of weekly worship.

The Roman Catholic Church has had a different problem in one respect, because preaching had to be restored to the Sunday mass in most parts of the Roman communion. The positive factor in this is that most Roman Catholic priests could start learning to preach from "scratch"; they didn't have to discard bad homiletical habits. For them, too, the Eucharist on Sunday was a "given." Although one Roman Catholic theologian said that preaching "is the most important thing the priest does in the mass" (Domenico Grasso, S.J., in *Proclaiming God's Message*), some observers believe that the preachers still have much to learn about preaching. One person wrote recently that he believes that not all who are called are able to learn to preach effectively. His solution is to invite lay people who have the gifts for preaching to participate in the preaching ministry of some churches. The Roman Catholic interest in homiletics places much emphasis upon the fundamentals of proclamation, as well the form of the sermon — and its delivery — *within the eucharistic setting*. The concern is with liturgical preaching.

In the last couple years, liturgiologists and homileticians have begun to speak and write about "holistic worship" and "holistic preaching." They simply mean that preaching and worship need to be considered together because they belong together, and that *all* dimensions of the two should be coordinated in planning worship and preaching within the liturgy. *The Song and the Story* is an effort to consider worship and preaching from such a holistic perspective, with stress upon holistic preaching of The Story.

1 The Song of the People of God

The Church of San Clemente, located about 300 yards from the Coliseum in Rome, is a graphic symbol of the contemporary liturgical renewal in the churches of Christendom. A place of public worship has continuously stood on that spot since late in the first century A.D. The present building was erected in the twelfth century, soon after the Normans had razed the edifice that had been built there after the Edict of Milan. That church, in turn, was constructed on the ruins of the home of Saint Clement, the third bishop of Rome. Clement's home had been destroyed during the terrible fire in A.D. 64, and apparently, in its reconstruction, a space was set aside for Christians to worship there; it was expanded into the "first" San Clemente. Today, San Clemente is an illustration of the continuity of Christian witness and worship in the world from the time of the Apostles to the present.

But San Clemente is more than a static representation of the development and continuity of liturgical worship; it is an excellent example of the evolution of Christian liturgy, not only in Rome but throughout the entire world in the intervening centuries. It stands over forty feet above the remains of Saint Clement's home, which was on the same level as the Coliseum. The character of the twelfth century building has, of course, changed due to renovation and some alteration, but the structure retains most of its original liturgical features, including some appointments from the fourth century church below it. A doorway in the sacristy opens into a staircase that leads down to the excavated nave and apse of the earlier edifice, upon which the twelfth century church was planned and placed. Another stairway (fourth century?) connects the lower building to the home of Saint Clement with its adjoining Mithraic "triclinium." Additional excavations have revealed another level of buildings dating to at least 500 B.C. The three levels of San Clemente are a demonstration of liturgical as well as architectural evolution in the Christian church, typifying what is happening in contemporary liturgical renewal as it moves backwards through the centuries and revises its liturgies from the perspective of past experience as well as present needs.[1]

The Renewal of the Song of God's People

Worship and the preaching that occur within the liturgical services of the churches are undergoing simultaneous renewal today in a manner that has occurred on such an extensive scale only twice before in the history of the Christian church. Liturgy and sermon were renewed simultaneously during the Reformation, especially in the Protestant churches but also in the Roman Catholic.[2] In the fourth century, when the churches moved their worship and liturgical activities from houses into church buildings, a similar and extensive overhauling of liturgies and preaching took place. By comparison, current attempts to revise and renew the worship and proclamation of the gospel in the churches seem more radical. In numerous buildings used for liturgical worship, altars — ornate or plain — stand neglected against the chancel walls of churches built for traditional rites, often replaced by simple tables close to, or in the middle of, the Christian assembly. Pastors often lead the liturgy from behind such free-standing altar-tables; some preach from the altar much as the fourth century bishops proclaimed the Word to their people "over the altar-table." Accordingly, some pulpits are physically empty — not psychologically "empty," as Clyde Reid described the estate of contemporary preaching a few years ago;[3] preachers influenced by communication theory and "experimental preaching" deliver their sermons from various locations within the worship space. Such physical changes testify to theological as well as practical developments in liturgies and homiletics.

The liturgical route to renewal, following Martin Luther's "lead" in the sixteenth century, lies in studying in depth the evolution of Christian worship. Adrian Nocent points out that, in the fourth century, as congregations moved their worship from houses into public buildings, liturgical elements were added to the worship to enable people to participate more fully in corporate devotional acts. Larger groups of people worshiping in more expansive spaces detracted from the participatory nature of worship in the smaller confines of Christian homes; the people had to be "rallied" in public worship, and, according to Nocent, liturgical changes were meant to accomplish this. But the Word was deemphasized in this liturgical process, opening the way for the emergence of ceremonialism, rubricism, and legalism within the liturgy.[4] "Surely the people had to be rallied," Nocent affirms, "but should they not have been rallied about the Word?" Rather than rallying people about the proclamation of the Word in the reading of the Bible, in the sermon that should be preached, and in the proclamation inherent in the Eucharist (1 Corinthians 11:26), emphasis was placed upon liturgical additions and details. Nocent observes: "We are faced with a paradox. Everything was done to rally the people . . . but the result was to diminish the importance of what was originally intended to unite them, the proclamation of the Word."[5] He calls rallying people about the Word the "pastoral principle" upon which valid and useful revision of the liturgy depends at any time. This was essentially what Luther had perceived almost four and a half centuries before Nocent wrote *The Future of the Liturgy* or Thomas Keir his version of *The Word in Worship*.[6] Liturgy that calls for proclamation of the Word in three modes — reading, speaking, and sacramental action — is established upon a firm and proper foundation in the Word of God that properly controls liturgical revision and homiletical change.

Word-centered worship, according to Thomas Keir, is "the Church's song as a vehicle of the Eternal Word."[7] The song is a response to God's revelation of himself — The Story — to his people, according to Keir:

> *When men encounter God redeemingly, the readiest and perhaps the veriest response is a song. And since it is doubt (occasioned by sin as doubt is) that is "our modern crown of thorns," the keynote of the exultation will be that this is primarily a believing and adoring song; it is characteristically a* Te Deum. Cantare amantis est, *which might be translated "a lover cannot help singing."*[8]

For Martin Luther, the Word means Jesus Christ who comes to people when the gospel is preached — and this leads to singing: "For 'gospel' (*Euangelicum*) is a Greek word and means, in Greek, a good message, good tidings, good news, a good report, which one sings and tells with gladness.'' Luther adds:

> *Thus this gospel of God or New Testament is a good story and report, sounded forth into all the world by the apostles, telling of a true David who strove with sin, death, and the devil, and overcame them, and thereby rescued all those who were captive in sin, afflicted with death, and overpowered by the devil. Without any merit of their own he made them righteous, gave them life, and saved them, so that they were given peace and brought back to God.* For this they sing, *and thank and praise God, and are glad forever . . .* [9]

Through the reading and preaching of the Word of God, Luther and the other Reformers "opened the mouths of the people who had been mostly silent in the place of worship for something like a thousand years. They permitted the liturgical song — the Scriptural psalms . . . and canticles . . . followed in course of time by Scriptural paraphrases, hymns, motets, and other sung parts of the service.''[10] Liturgical revision today has much of the same intention — to enable people to sing their song of praise and thanksgiving to God in response to his gracious gift, Jesus Christ. These efforts have to be, and are, gospel-centered liturgies of Word (and Sacrament). *The Son is the congregation's extension of the Story.*

How Liturgies Are Changing

In his version of *The Word in Worship,* William Skudlarek spoke to many of the liturgical-homiletical issues raised by Thomas Keir and others about the need for reform, pointing out the problems of Roman Catholics and Protestants in worship. He writes:

The past generation of Roman Catholics and Protestants experienced, for the most part, a form of worship that was a mere torso — a sacramental service without preaching, a preaching service without the sacrament. Today that regretable maiming is being healed.[11]

And he adds, " . . . we can be grateful that the church today seems well on the way to redressing the distortion of its worship that has been centuries in the making."[12] In effect, the Common Service of the Christian Church has been revised by Roman Catholics and Protestants alike so that Roman Catholics will be encouraged to restore preaching to the Sunday mass and Protestants will alter the Protestant Preaching Service by including the celebration of the Eucharist in normal Sunday worship. It is just possible that the Roman Catholics, so far, have had more success than Lutherans, Episcopalians, Methodists, and other Protestants in liturgical-homiletical reform. Roman Catholic priests are required to preach in the Sunday mass; Protestant pastors and their congregations have no such liturgical mandates placed upon them to include the Sacrament of the Altar as part of every Sunday's liturgy. For example, both the new worship books of American Lutherans, *Lutheran Book of Worship* and *Lutheran Worship,* make provision for those Sundays when "there is no communion." Both make provision for a formal and liturgical Protestant Preaching Service. The formal preaching service is not quite "dead."

Most of the new Sunday, or Eucharistic, liturgies highlight the Word (or, as it was known, the *Synaxis).* The emphasis might fall, for instance, on the reading and preaching of the gospel. The majority of these versions of the Common Service places the Creed and the Hymn of the Day *after* the sermon so that the lessons flow quickly and naturally into the sermon without any break. The reading of the Holy Gospel from the pulpit, just before the sermon is preached, is an increasingly common phenomenon in many liturgical — Catholic and Protestant — churches. The sermon is situated in the first half of the worship hour, rather than in the last half, as in the typical Protestant Preaching Service. The sequence of lessons and sermon makes it abundantly clear that the preacher should employ the Holy Gospel, and/or the other lessons, as the preaching text. This is a fundamental precept of liturgical preaching; so-called "free-choice" texts for preaching find no place in this Sunday worship-preaching pattern simply because they usually intrude upon the unity of the Word in liturgy, lessons, and sermon.

And more of The Story is to be read in worship through the expansion of the one-year lectionary into a three-year system for reading the Scriptures to the people. The mandate of Vatican II upon Roman Catholic biblical and liturgical scholars to "open up more of the Bible" for the people in public worship was responsible — after considerable study, consultation with Protestant scholars, and experimentation — for the development of a three-year lectionary with each year's lections arranged around one of the synoptic gospels. A two-year lectionary was rejected because it would have been too restrictive, while a four-year lectionary, it was concluded, would have proven too repetitive. The Gospel of John would remain — in all three years — as the gospel for the Easter season and, to a lesser degree, for Lent. The semicontinuous reading of the gospel through about sixty percent of the year and the second lessons (the Epistles) during Epiphany and Pentecost is evolutionary in nature, as William Skudlarek explains in his *The Word in Worship*.[13] *The Bible is read as a story.*

The emphasis upon the corporate nature of worship, which is built into the new liturgies by changes in language, music, prayers, and dialogue, is another result of liturgical revision. All of the people — not just the pastor — are to be active participants in liturgical worship. Corporate worship is the liturgical order of the day; *all* should hear the Word, sing the song, say the prayers, and give thanks to God for his grace. But liturgical worship is no free-for-all wherein anyone does what they feel like doing, even if they are prompted, in their own minds, by the Holy Spirit:

> *To participate, we now realize, does not mean doing and reciting everything that the priest (or preacher) does and recites. There is in the Christian assembly a function for each one . . . the celebrant has his, just as the ministers, the servers, and the faithful have theirs. This participation is not isolated and personal; it takes place in the very heart of the Christian community, and this close association of all the members in the Eucharistic meeting ought to be tangibly signified and experienced.*[14]

The role of the pastor is to be the presider and preacher, opening and closing the liturgy, leading in the prayers at the altar-table, and controlling the liturgy so that the people may participate harmoniously and meaningfully. When the pastors proclaim the Word, the people preach through them.

James Huston could have been talking about the role of the preacher in liturgical worship, instead of a pianist, Roy Ambrose, in his story, *Gig.* Roy invites people to sit around the piano, to join him in duets, sing along with him, or just whistle. Through Roy Ambrose, Huston makes his social — and liturgical — commentary:

> *For thousands of years we've been stuck with this notion of one man getting up on the stage* or

in the pulpit (emphasis mine), *on his high horse before some mute multitude — one actor or juggler or tap dancer or novelist or professor or minister up there doing his act, while everybody else watches, immobilized voyeurs. When the truth is . . . "Everybody wants to get into the act." And why not, I want to know. Why continue this conspiracy of performers to keep the audience in its place? . . . Why not let everybody get into the act?*[15]

Liturgical worship as the "work of the people" requires, if it is to be done properly and in response to the Word, that "everybody should get into the act," but the ordained minister is to preside over the entire worship service. Roy Ambrose, in *Gig,* could have been speaking for liturgical "presiders" when he "hastens to add, . . . as long as I am in charge."

Protestant congregations seem to be adjusting more rapidly to the concept of corporate worship than they are to the celebration of the weekly Eucharist. Herbert Lindemann correctly concludes, "Little by little the idea has gained ground that worship is a corporate act, in which other people besides the pastor have parts to play. . . ."[16] And as people are discovering the corporate character of worship, they are gradually learning the importance of the full eucharistic liturgy to provide the most viable means of full and satisfying participation in Christian worship. Adult study classes seldom study theology as abstract thought today, but make the concrete associations of "new accents," as Eugene Brand calls them, in liturgy and life — "the spirit of thanksgiving" in the ecumenical emphasis on the Eucharist, as well as Sacrifice, Real Presence, and Eschatology. Brand insists that this combination of theological understanding restores the concept of the Christian Church as a "pilgrim people" who are underway "from resurrection to parousia, from Baptism to death/ resurrection . . ." And, he declares, "Once caught, that orientation will turn the meal into a true Eucharist and save it from the lugubriousness and legalism of the 'commissary mentality' [which exists, he asserts] in some congregations."[17] Nor is the Eucharist a "spiritual first-aid station from which the faithful may draw upon "a storehouse of grace" when in desperate need. By ecumenical consensus, the Eucharist is — and ought to be again in every congregation — a "shared celebration" of the grace of God that makes us new and hopeful creatures in Jesus Christ while attempting to live faithfully in a world that is in danger of falling apart or blowing itself to pieces.

The mainline churches of Christendom have, for the most part, become aware of the relationship between liturgy and doctrine and theology *(Lex orandi-Lex credendi)* which Toivo Harjunpaa referred to as an "old phrase . . . which expresses a vital truth so often neglected among us. This phrase proclaims the truth that there exists a relationship of cause and effect between the ordered prayer, i.e., the public worship and the official creeds and dogmatic formulations of the church."[18] This much is clear to all who investigate why and how the worship of the church is changing: The evolution of liturgical worship in the Christian church is, and has been, influenced by three factors — the historical, the theological, and the pastoral.[19] This combination has changed, and will continue to exert pressure toward revision of, liturgical worship.

Liturgy and the Preaching of the Word

The problems with preaching, as they were expounded by Clyde Reid[20] during the period when liturgical experimentation was beginning in the churches, are not resolved with the appearance of new liturgies and lectionaries, or even by a flood of exegetical-homiletical "helps." If anything, the liturgical renewal complicates the business of preaching within the liturgy of the church. Roman Catholics might be in danger of over-emphasizing the mechanics of preaching and the acquisition of communication skills as they concentrate on learning how to preach again, but Protestants run the risk of stressing *the content of the biblical sermon to the neglect of its shape.* The liturgy calls for a sermon, not a lesson or a lecture on the Bible, theology, or any other subject. The shape, as well as the biblical content, of a sermon is of critical importance to effective preaching. So Thomas Keir, when he discusses the "problem of language," asks an important question of preachers: "What is it that marks the difference between a good theological essay and a good sermon?" He replies for the preachers:

> *We all know the answer. It is that a good the-ological essay is a helpful arrangement and criti-cism of ideas with a view to better understanding of some objective truth, while a sermon, though it ought to be built on this, is something more, something different. It is going into action.* [21]

Keir parallels Luther's "My tongue is the pen of a ready writer" and his emphasis upon the oral communication of the Word: "And the gospel should really not be something written, but a spoken word which brought forth the Scriptures, as Christ and the Apostles have done." Luther insisted that the gospel "is spread not by pen but by word of mouth." [22]

And so the preacher within the revised liturgies must be, preeminently, a proclaimer of the Word in the classic "mode," giving a "face" to Word and Sacrament through the proclamation of the gospel. The announcement of the Good News remains — and will continue to be — the most important action of the preacher within the worship of the church. *Preaching has been elevated,* not eliminated or diminished, by the call to corporate and eucharistic worship, and the preachers must speak the Word with boldness and precision, addressing both the spiritual needs and the ministry of the people in the world. Effective preaching moves people to renewal at the Lord's Table and into the world to serve in Jesus' name. The reading of the lections without a sermon, while suitable for some auxiliary services, is asking the Bible to do too much in worship. Beyond interpretation and application of the Word, preaching — and preachers — are faced with the necessity of *speaking the Word* from the vantage point of personal faith; it is an affirmation — "I believe!" And such proclamation, when gospel-oriented, allows God to *speak* through his called and ordained servants.

Preaching is an oral event. I once knew a preacher who had a number of hard-of-hearing persons in his congregation — and no amplification system or hearing aids. One member suggested that the pastor should give him and the hearing impaired people copies of his sermon outline before he preached the message. He complied with the suggestion, only to discover that others in the congregation also wanted the outlines in advance. Before he knew it, he was distributing his outline, then the entire written sermon with the Sunday bulletin. In time, he wondered why the people didn't seem to be listening to his sermons as they had in the past, as well as why there was little or no response to them. Preaching has to take its cue from Sir Walter Scott's incisive lines in *The Heart of Midlothian.* When Jeannie Deans announces her intention to make the long journey from Edinburgh to London to plead with the Queen for the life of her condemned sister, she is asked, "Why not send a letter?" She replies, "A letter canna do it. A letter canna look and beg and beseech as the human voice can do to the human heart . . . The word of maun (mouth) must do it, or naething else.''[23] The Word must be spoken — *effectively* — in the sermon if the gospel is to have its full impact on the people. Then they will sing the song as they participate in the action of the liturgy, not only in the worship service but in the world.

The Problem of Sermon-Shape

But how can the sermon be shaped so that its content will be biblical and, specifically, gospel-oriented and, at the same time fit the revised liturgy while also accommodating good communication theory? The emphasis upon "experimental preaching" to improve oral communication of the Word from the pulpit, begun in the 1960s, continues, but liturgy and its integral parts have been "set" for almost a decade in many of the denominations of the Christian Church in the West. John Killinger is correct in his observation:

A profusion of homiletical theory is now pouring forth, but without consensus. The secure old positions and rationales of Broadus and Sangster no longer cast their freezing shadows over neophyte preachers — the former are indeed almost unknown to the latter.[24]

When the liturgy is recognized for what it is — the worship of God's people gathered together to hear and celebrate The Story of that loving relationship he has established and maintains with them in Jesus Christ through the Word and the Holy Spirit — *a consensus about the nature and shape of preaching may be achieved.* Just as the lectionary ought to be understood as the reading of The Story in public worship, so should preaching be comprehended as *telling The Story* to the believers assembled in the name of the Lord.

The homiletical dilemma is more than a somewhat confusing struggle on the part of preachers to discover — or invent — shapes for sermons that will insure imaginative communication of the gospel; rather, it is fundamentally a matter of comprehending the nature of Christian worship in the liturgy and the role of preaching within it; form follows function. Evolution in worship and preaching after the Reformation altered the ancient liturgy of the Word. Reading, preaching, and proclaiming the Word were removed from the Eucharist into a truncated preaching service (among Protestants) in which the Sacrament of the Altar was celebrated only occasionally. As worship changed, so did the shape of the sermon. Roman Catholics, following 1570 and the counter-Reformation, forgot about preaching, as William Skudlarek and others admit, and tended to concentrate on the aesthetic and ceremonial aspects of liturgical worship. Both groups need to restore preaching within eucharistic worship, and both need to settle upon a theology of liturgical preaching which will inform the actual shape, or shapes, that the sermon takes within worship. Simply to restore the weekly Eucharist in Protestant worship will not alter the shape of the sermon or even make the worship more corporate in character, nor will restoration of the sermon to the Catholic mass guarantee that the Word will be preached with power and usefulness for God's people. The preaching problem is more complicated than that; even story preaching, the latest homiletical emphasis, will not solve it by itself. The Story, as read and preached, needs to become again — as in the early church — the basis of the Song of the Christians who respond with thanksgiving and praise to God for his grace in Jesus Christ as well as an integral part of The Song, the liturgy of the Christian Church. The study of the evolution of worship in the early centuries of Christianity informs us today that this is possible when worship becomes corporate again through the reading, preaching, and eucharistic proclamation of the Word as The Story.

The Church of San Clemente shows us the evolution that has occurred in Christian worship and takes us back through the centuries to worship in the house-churches. Its lesson is that the Word must be the primary element in Christian worship. The Word must be read as The Story, preached as The Story, and celebrated as The Story. Then the people who sing The Story as a song in their worship will tell it to the world through loving service and ministry.

2 Reading the Story

Every church building is a repository of stories which are lived out by people, told and retold again and again. They are stories of the encounter between God and his people in and through Jesus Christ. The great cathedrals of Europe have always had stories told in them and about the people who built, supported, and worshiped in them. The Cathedral of Notre Dame in Paris has contributed its share of such stories to the literature of the church and the world and, specifically, to preaching.

In the middle of the thirteenth century, while Notre Dame was still under construction, a storyteller named Rutebeuf — "Rough Ox" — acted out one of his tales for the congregation — this one a retelling of the ancient story of Theophilus cast in the mold of a miracle play. It was especially appropriate for the Church of Our Lady because, through a "miracle of miracles," she accomplished the defeat of Satan and the subsequent release of Theophile, as he was named at that time, from the clutches of the Devil.

Rutebeuf could be a comic, a clown, or one who would cajole the audience, but in "one matter Reutebeuf was serious to the point of gravity: his belief in Mary." He was convinced that she had the power to work miracles and, especially, to defeat Satan. His play was really a statement of his faith in God through the work of the Virgin Mary. At the close of the play, the restored Theophilus is "perched on the edge of his (bishop's) throne as he speaks:

Hear, for the sake of God, Mary's Son,
Good people, the true-life lesson
 of Theophile,
Whom the Enemy tricked by guile.
As clear as Blessed Evangel
 Is this thing.
Immaculate Virgin Mary
Saved him from such a quandary.
And now for this delivery,
 Let us all rise,
Singing: "O Lord to Thee our Praise."[1]

Allen Temko, who recreated and retells this story, imagines that "Notre Dame echoed triumphant music, taking it upward in buttress and arch, and through the transept spire to Heaven. The Church became a great *Te Deum* in itself."

This story is connected to an earlier tale of how St. Dominic Domingo de Guzman "prayed passionately to Mary shortly after 1200, at the time St. Francis was preaching to the birds at Assisi." According to the story, "in a blinding flash of light,"

the image on the altar came to life, as it did in the play for Theophile. The Virgin opened a Bible and gave Dominic the text for his sermon. Whereupon the founder of the Dominican Order made his way back through the sanctuary, past the tombs of prelates and princes, including the

> *gilded copper sarcophagus of Eudes de Sully*
> *(bishop of Paris at the time construction began*
> *on Notre Dame), to the entrance of the choir to*
> *address the people in the nave.* [2]

And so the Dominican Order, the great preaching order
of the Roman Catholic Church, was born through —
and has been, to some extent, perpetuated by — an
encounter-story.

Domingo must have made at least a portion of that
sermon into a personal narrative, which he told over
and over to clergy and laity alike. He might have said,
"The Virgin, just now in a vision, gave me this text.
Here's how it happened . . ." — and a narrative
sermon, in part, at least, came into being. That story
must have been as moving an experience for the congregation that day as was Rutebeuf's play about the Virgin
Mary some sixty years later. Narrative preaching
received fresh stimulus through St. Dominic's experience, based on the Word of God and not simply upon
the mystical experience of the founder of the Dominican
Order. The Dominicans today, with most of the liturgical churches of Christendom, base their sermons on a
system — the church year and lectionary — that selects
lessons for worship and preaching.

The Lectionary: Selections from the Story

When the New Testament books were written down
and used in worship along with the Old Testament, the
Bible was read as a story within a calendar year. Genesis
1 was read on Septuagesima Sunday and continued to be
read in the daily worship until it was completed. Exodus
and the other books followed until the entire Bible was
read during the year. That method of reading Scripture
gave way by the Middle Ages to the pericope/church
year system of assigning texts to Sundays and festivals.

The current lectionary scheme combines both methods for reading the Bible in public worship; three of the four Gospels are read as continuing stories in a semicontinuous manner, and the epistles follow the same plan for most of the year. The Old Testament lections are selected to harmonize with the Gospel for the Day* and most of them, like the gospels, are stories of the faith — how God has dealt with his creation and his children, and how they have reacted to him and to each other.

The lectionary ought to be thought of as the "story book of the church," particularly in conjunction with the gospels. On Sundays and the festivals of the year the Story of Jesus is read as the climactic scripture reading of the day or feast. Arndt Halvorson, a colleaque, stated in an unpublished lecture: "Through the big Story God entered the world; through the little stories God entered our lives."[3] The "big Story" of the redeeming events initiated by the Father in Christ is read on the principal festivals of the Christian calendar; the "little stories" (in the pericopes) are read on the Sundays of the year. Through the reading of the Bible in this way the "story of Jesus" — the gospel — is thrust into a primary role in Christian worship. The most important parts of the Story are read over a three-year period, and then are repeated again in this ongoing three-year cycle of scripture readings. The worship of the church, the preaching of the Word, and the faith of the people rest firmly on the Holy Scriptures rather than on contemporary topics or tradition. The lectionary insists that Christian worship must be biblical.

The great festivals of Christ — Christmas, Easter, Pentecost — are shaped by the stories that are read as

---

*A proposed "Common Lectionary" would change the character of Old Testament readings, allowing them to stand independent of the gospel readings.

they are anticipated and celebrated. The beloved stories about the birth of Jesus, his life, ministry, suffering and death, and resurrection generate wonder and excitement among the listeners when they are read in proper sequence during the year. The story they tell has power inherent in it — sometimes even without preaching — to evoke faith and trust in God. That power has been experienced by untold numbers of people who have read the Story for themselves, and when the Story is read aloud in a Christian assembly — as it is meant to be read — the impact is just as great, or greater. The "old, old Story" retains its ability to move people to repentance and faith.

The genius of the lectionary is that the first and second lessons, as well as the Holy Gospel, were chosen for their "gospel content" rather than for doctrinal foundations or ethical emphases. Luther understood gospel this way, especially in connection with the whole Testament. In his *A Brief Instruction on What to Look For and Expect in the Gospels,* he wrote:

> *It is a common practice to number the gospels and to name them by books and say that there are four gospels. From this practice stems the fact that no one knows what St. Paul and St. Peter are saying in their epistles, and their teaching is regarded as an addition to the gospels . . . One should thus realize that there is only one gospel, but that it is described by many apostles. Every single epistle of Paul and of Peter, as well as the Acts of the Apostles by Luke, is a gospel, even though they do not record all the works and words of Christ, but one is shorter and includes less than another. There is not one of the four major gospels anyway that includes all the words and works of Christ; nor is this necessary.* [4]

In another writing, *Prefaces to the New Testament,* he adds: "Therefore it should be known . . . that the notion must be given up that there are four gospels and only four evangelists . . . so the New Testament is a book in which are written the gospel and the promises of God, together with a history of those who believe and of those who do not believe them."[5]

For Luther, the Old Testament was not gospel, but a "book in which are written God's laws and commandments, together with a history of those who kept and of those who did not keep them . . . "[6] Luther might not accept the concept of gospel in the Old Testament, because he applies the term strictly to Christ, and he might not be pleased with the "Year of Matthew," "Year of Mark," "Year of Luke" arrangement in view of his opinion about the value of those three gospels over against the Gospel of John and the epistles of St. Peter and St. Paul,[7] but he would be pleased with that fact that John is the most used New Testament book in the "consensus lectionary" and that Romans is the work among the epistles most often employed as a second lesson. He believed that these two books told the story of Christ — the gospel — better than any of the other books of the New Testament. Luther will never allow us to forget that the gospel is the story — and only one story — about Jesus Christ. The three-year lectionary we use, even though of Roman Catholic origin, attests to the enduring value of Luther's opinion in regard to the church's public worship, especially regarding scripture reading and preaching.

The Lectionary and the Liturgy

The genius of the liturgy as it employs the lectionary (and church year) in worship is that by highlighting the reading of one of the four gospels the entire service of worship becomes Christ-centered. And the liturgy does this by making the Gospel for the Day the chief lesson; it is always read as the third lesson, the "dominant" lesson of the liturgical occasion. And while the first lesson always is meant to harmonize with the theme of the gospel, during approximately thirty-five percent to forty percent of the year (Advent, Christmas, Lent, Easter, and all festivals), first and second lessons "graduate" into the gospel. Thus the life of Jesus Christ, from before his birth to his ascension, is reviewed and his Story is retold by the readings (and sermons) and at least part of the Story is reenacted every Sunday in the Eucharist. "Our job, as preachers," says Arndt Halvorson, "is to help people see the big Story in the light of the little portion of it, the pericopes."[8] *Thus, the perspective from which we proclaim any of the lessons in the lectionary is kergymatic.*

Simply because the liturgy recognizes that the gospel is a story, not merely a "third lesson" (the formula for introducing the gospel is always "Holy Gospel" and never "lesson"), it seems to be reminding preachers that preaching is always *telling the Story* and not teaching a lesson. Thus, the liturgy informs the preacher about the form best suited to the proclamation of the person and work of Jesus Christ, the biblical story sermon rather than other types of biblical sermons. Many preachers take for granted that the best shape for biblical preaching is the expository sermon without realizing that at least five types of expository sermon-shapes are in existence and used by various preachers. Evidence in printed sermons and conversations with numerous pastors indicate they choose the expository style because it seems best suited for teaching from the pulpit. "After all," a great number asks, "if I don't teach on Sunday morning, when will I be able to reach the greatest number of my people?" They assume that the lessons of the lectionary *should be taught*, not simply told.

But preachers ought not make hasty decisions about using didactic sermon shapes simply on the basis of homiletical theory; they need to take the revised liturgy, as well as the lectionary, into consideration, remembering that the first half of the liturgy, which is often called "the Office of the Word," is different from the *missa catechumenorum* (which Luther inherited and reformed in the sixteenth century). Today's liturgy calls for announcement of the Word, proclamation of the gospel, or preaching the Story of Jesus, and not for pulpit-teaching of the Bible. Preachers ought also to realize that didactic preaching is always risky business, difficult to do well under most circumstances. Too many preachers are locked into this type of preaching, according to Richard Jensen, who observes: "Ninety percent of the preaching I hear and probably ninety percent of the preaching that I have done is essentially didactic in character . . . What I would like to maintain is that didactic preaching dominates the present homiletical world . . . "⁹

Jensen has developed what he calls "Gutenberg homiletics" to point out the characteristics in didactic preaching that call for other types of sermons. These are:

1. The goal of preaching is to teach the lessons of the text.

2. In order to teach the lessons or meaning of the text, the points to be made are usually abstracted from the text.

3. The sermon is aimed primarily at the hearer's mind.

4. The sermon is developed in a logical, sequential and linear manner.

5. The sermon is prepared under the criteria for

written material.

6. The faith engendered in the hearer is "faith" that the ideas are true.[10]

His goal is to encourage didactic preachers to rethink their preaching methodology so that they change to an oral style that will radically alter the shape of their sermons. His goal is to convince preachers to attempt — occasionally, at least — to prepare and preach story sermons.

The liturgy, by its very nature, suggests that liturgical sermons ought to be clear, and uncomplicated, and uncluttered — like a good story. The whole liturgy is constructed around Jesus and his story, not around the concept of a "worship experience." The reading and preaching of the Word are intended to reach us where we are, convict us, turn us to Christ and edify us, and send us to the table where he is host, renewing our baptismal covenant in his Body and Blood and reconciling us to God our Father. The Eucharist is a sacrament, not a seance. It gives us the opportunity to participate in Jesus' story in our Christian assembly and liturgy instead of simply listening to a sermon, making our offering, lifting our prayers to God, and, perhaps, going on our way rejoicing. When the sermon tells the Story, there is a good chance that the response, especially in the Holy Communion, will be immediate participation in the life offered by the risen Christ.

James W. Cox is right when he states that the renewal in worship has made an impact upon preaching that calls for change in the shape of the sermon;

If the worship setting is agreeable *(emphasis, mine), the sermon may be monologue, a dialogue, a trialogue, a drama, a film, a multi-media presentation, or some other form of preaching that answers to a need. In fact, the very style of the liturgy may dictate the form of the sermon.*[11]

He parallels Richard Jensen's concern for change and variety in the form of the sermon:

> *I am pleased when I hear of a preacher who seeks and can find opportunities to do something different — so different that he can break through the crust of indifference that characterizes so many gospel-hardened worshipers.*[12]

The style of the Sunday liturgy — the Eucharist — does not encourage as much experimentation in sermon-shaping as Cox might like to see preachers attempt. The eucharistic liturgy employed by many churches on Sundays suggests, if it does not "dictate," some kind of a story sermon in the preaching. Liturgy, lectionary, plus the church year, when they are considered as a "kerygmatic combination" that informs preachers about the proclamation of the gospel, call for biblical preaching that tells the Story and, through our "little stories," involves us in it.

Worship and the Church Year

The proclamation of the gospel inspires the song that God's people sing, as Luther and others have noted, and which has taken the shape that we call liturgy. One liturgical element — the church year — serves both worship and preaching as it signals presider and preacher — and the people — concerning the biblical orientation of celebration and procla-mation. Frequently called the calendar of the church, it enables the church to "tell time" from the perspective of what God has done in the world — and what he does now and will do in the future — in Jesus Christ. Structured as it is about the major events in the life of Jesus Christ — *the kerygma*, as C. H. Dodd called them — the church (or Christian) year might be called the kerygmatic timepiece of the Christian Church. It reminds God's faithful people about extraordinary moments in time, but it also establishes a rhythm of worship in ordinary time which creates a "flow of time" — *chronos* — from past to present to the "last things" within the plan of God. Rachel Reeder, in an issue of *Liturgy* devoted to the calendar, writes:

> *We live between two ages always, and the seasons are always changing, but they, and we, are centered in the mystery of redemption. That is our point of equilibrium; the father of Jesus is the Lord of Time. Let there be no mistake — we cannot live the struggles of yesterday's church and saints, but we can share the intensity of the desire to find a meaning, purpose, and style of life that will survive the risks of evil and sin.*[13]

The calendar zeroes in on the new creation God began when the Kingdom of God broke into time. It fills us with hope because the fulness of that Kingdom is yet to come through the return and triumphant reign of Jesus Christ.

Rachel Reeder almost understates the case when she comments: "It takes only a few minutes to read the general norms on the church year in the new worship books; it will take much longer to realize their depth."[14] As a calendar it directs the church when — and what — to celebrate in its life in Christ. As a hermeneutical framework formed about the lectionary and the liturgy, it insists on theological interpretation of those gospel events that are celebrated. We begin to plumb the depths of the church year when the birth of Christ is put forth as incarnation, when his death and resurrection are pictured — especially in preaching — as redemption and justification, when his ascension and promised return are interpreted as glorification and parousia. The hermeneutical framework, ultimately, is eschatological, especially in the liturgy as a "foretaste of the feast to come" and "a proclamation of his death until he comes again."

The church year discourages preaching within the liturgy to be an exercise in exegesis or Bible study that attempts to take the hearers back to another time and place and locates the religious experience of people today in the past. Gerard S. Sloyan insists on an eschatological stance in liturgical preaching:

> *Appeals to the past (in liturgy and proclamation) as such, even the sacred past, are so much lost time. The mood must always be contemporary if it is to succeed . . . even in the most traditional religious cultures . . . Relevance has to do with what applies properly to the matter at hand . . .*

He adds, "The liturgy, the preaching that looks to yesterday and backward and not to today and forward is archaeology; a symphony of dead forms."[15] And so, the church year, properly understood, establishes and maintains an eschatological "mood," as Sloyan would likely call it, for both worship and preaching. Unless preaching, in particular, is cast in this eschatological dimension when the gospel-story is told, there is little point in preaching at all in a world like ours. The end of the Story is yet to be told — by God and in Christ — but it has been promised, and it will surely come at the appointed time.

The Church Year and Planning One's Preaching

One of the blessings of the ecumenical lectionary is that sermon planning and preparation have been given new impetus. Denominational and interdenominational lectionary study groups have sprung up in numerous committees; pastors study the Sunday pericopes a week or two before they will be read in worship and employed as preaching texts. This means that there is long-term hope for the future of the Christian Church; when pastors study God's Word together, feasting upon the story of his faithfulness and grace, allowing Christ and the Spirit to instruct them, they just might discover their unity in Christ and his church. But the immediate results will be evident in the sermons that they are preaching; regarding content, at least, the preaching in liturgically-oriented churches has to be improving, and we can hope it will continue to improve.

Whether or not preachers participate in homiletical study groups, each preacher still has to prepare his or her own sermon and preach it. Lectionary or nonlectionary related preaching, to be effective, requires some sort of Sunday-to-Sunday procedure, or system, that takes advantage of time available each day of the week. The systematic use of time for sermon preparation is critical in sermon planning and production, and there simply is not enough time to prepare during the week if the preacher does not have a preaching system to follow. Preachers may belong to lectionary study groups, but they still have to do their own hard work and that begins with the reading of the Sunday texts — as a story — allowing the gospel story to come to life in the mind and heart. Each preacher has to do that in private, in the study. Arndt Halvorson adds his voice to that of Donald Miller, Andrew Blackwood and other homileticians when he insists:

So our first step in the sermon is to read the text
— in English. Don't begin as an historical, gram-
matical, literary, theological researcher. Neither
begin as a contemporary sociologist and psychol-
ogist. Begin *the task as a human being who*
happens to be living in the early twilight of the
twentieth century, who now must deal with these
words as if they made the difference between life
and death. So read, read, and re-read the text.[16]

It was this type of study of the Scriptures, according to
Andrew Blackwood, that transformed Thomas
Chalmers from an ordinary to an extraordinary pro-
claimer of the Word.

In the first six years or so of his parish ministry,
Chalmers gave no promise of becoming an outstanding
preacher. He had a friend, John, who visited him quite
often and said to him one day, "Whenever I come (to
see you), you are always busy but not with your prep-
arations for the Sabbath." To which Chalmers replied,
"An hour or two on the Saturday eve is quite enough
for that." But then Chalmers began to preach with
power; with Luther he had discovered the Bible and had
begun really to explore it. After this change had taken
place in Chalmer's preaching ministry, his friend John
observed: "Now, sir, whenever I come, I always find
you at your Bible." And Chalmers is reported to have
said, "All too little, John. All too little."[17]

Halvorson gives some excellent advice to preachers
on how they ought to read the biblical texts as preaching
texts in a section of his book, *Authentic Preaching*. He
believes that the preacher should read the text "as if it
were a clue to the whole story. Read it as a detective who
has found a relevant but unclear scrap of paper in the
wastebasket of the dead person's room." The text ought
to be read "for its concreteness," "with reverence,"
"as the symbol you have to make room for in your

imagination," "as a *story* — or part of a story," "for the tone of the discourse," and "as one involved in it *personally.*" After this approach to beginning the sermon — and only after this advice — does Professor Halvorson proceed to the other matters involved in preparing the sermon, "from text to sermon."[18]

Homiletical Planning

The church-year pericope system takes us to another level of dealing with the lectionary texts — reading *and planning* one's preaching from the perspective of the Christian year; this gives an additional dimension to one's sermon preparation. Good sermons take time to germinate, to grow, and to mature. Andrew Blackwood believed that effective preaching could only be achieved through *long-term planning* and effort through the use of what he called "a sermonic seed plot" — a protracted preaching plan. He taught a course in "Planning the Year's Pulpit Work" — and wrote extensively about it. He believed that such planning is of utmost importance in the parish homiletical process. I fully concur with him and others who have seen the wisdom of such preaching procedures.

The church year offers preachers an almost ready-made, long-term plan for one's preaching ministry. The three cycles and six seasons, together with the greater and lesser festivals, situate sermon planning and production in a broader perspective than is possible if the preacher works only on a week-by-week, or Sunday-to-Sunday basis. It encourages preachers to work within the scope of the whole Story before dealing with portions of it as the Lectionary excises them and appoints them to the Sundays and festivals of the year. It urges preachers to read all of the lessons of the year before — preferably long before — the First Sunday in Advent. It intimates that the "gospel of the year" should be read through, perhaps at one reading — and at least a second time — before the critical work of exegesis and the tedious business of preparing the weekly sermons begin. The church year is a ready-made "sermonic seed plot" whose soil is rich beyond compare because that soil is the sacred Scriptures that culminate in the story of Jesus Christ.

Planning by the Cycles

The church year has a plan-within-a-plan built into it that can be of considerable assistance to preachers as they attempt to develop a long-term plan. It is in the two sanctoral cycles, Christmas and Easter, and the long temporal cycle, Pentecost. By dividing the Pentecost season into a summer portion and a fall section — for planning purposes — preachers avail themselves of what amounts to a four-cycle system for sermon planning and sermon production. The system accommodates worship planning, as well.

Advent, Christmas, and Epiphany constitute the Christmas cycle. Since Advent is always a season of four Sundays' duration and the Christmas season is twelve days long, the addition of the old *gesima* Sundays to Epiphany creates a cycle that is approximately three months in length. In some years the cycle will be exactly thirteen weeks long, but it will always be approximately one quarter of the calendar year. But more important, if preachers plan their sermons for the entire cycle rather than for one Sunday at a time or even for a season, the themes of their preaching ministry will be coordinated with each other and reflect the motifs of the church as well.

Lent and Easter are always thirteen weeks in length; Lent includes six Sundays (six and a half weeks from Ash Wednesday to Holy Saturday), and Easter always has seven weeks in its season. This never varies; the

Easter cycle is always one quarter of the year. By planning one's preaching for the complete cycle, one not only develops a more comprehensive plan, but the preacher is given the opportunity to deal with two of the most obvious weaknesses of Lent-Easter preaching. First, Lent will be cast into its proper role in the cycle as a season of preparation for the celebration of Christ's resurrection, and Easter will receive proper emphasis as the "essential season"[19] of the church year. Lent, as now understood and celebrated in most churches, tends to overshadow the "great fifty days" of Easter. The recovery of Easter in the worship of our churches could make a marked difference in the lives of the people of God. Preaching in this cycle connects our "little stories" to the "big Story" of Jesus Christ and proclaims the "whole" Story.

Second, with a more definitive study of the structure and purposes of Lent, the "assumed" themes will yield to the "actual" and intended themes of the season. The forty days of Lent are, as is commonly supposed, given over only to the Passion of Christ; the passion is properly assigned to the last week of Lent, now known as "the Week of the Passion." The first five and a half weeks of Lent remain penitential in character, but an existential thrust — new to most twentieth-century Christians — is given this portion of Lent (and Easter, too). Lent becomes a time when all Christians are to die with Christ in Baptism and to renew their baptismal covenant in the Easter event of cross and empty tomb. Lent is the period when the faithful approach the cross to participate in his death; Easter means resurrection with the Lord as a "new creation" and results in living out the new life in Christ. Thus, Lent and Easter can become — when worship and, especially, preaching are cycle-oriented — the pattern for daily living, "dying and rising daily with Christ" (Luther). Baptism is the fulcrum on which rests our experience of the Easter event, as well as the means by which the right relationship of Lent and Easter can be restored. Preaching planned within this kind of a sacramentally-related cycle should be radically different from — and more biblically and theologically oriented than — planning done separately for Lent and Easter.

For sermon planning purposes, the season of Pentecost presents another set of problems. Revised, as it is, in name only, it is still too long and thematically shapeless; its hermeneutical framework seems rather fragile. Sunday, the little Easter, sounds the clearest kerygmatic note among the signals that are indistinct and uncertain; the days of saints and martyrs amplify it.[20] But, in Pentecost, the reading of the "Gospel of the Year" comes into its own through the semicontinuous reading of Matthew, Mark, and Luke in their appointed turns. The gospels set the themes for each of the weeks of Pentecost, but within the "time of the Church" (as this season has been described).

Preachers would do well to divide their Pentecost preaching-planning into two parts of approximately equal length — a summer section stretching from Pentecost to the end of August and a fall portion from the beginning of September to the Festival of Christ the King close to the end of November. In such a plan, Labor Day becomes the dividing point in Pentecost, replacing the festivals of SS. Peter and Paul (June 29), St. Lawrence (August 10), and St. Michael and All Angels (September 29), which anciently separated the season into four sections. Divided into two parts, the church year not only gives preachers four cycles, but provides for planning that will accommodate the two radically different situations (summer and fall) which preaching has to address during Pentecost.

A four-part preaching plan of this kind, when put into action before each cycle begins, allows preachers adequate time to study the gospel in detail, as well as do preliminary reading, research, and exegesis, and develop the sermon ideas for each Sunday of the cycle. A short-term plan for each week of the year leads to the final preparation and production of the sermon to be preached that week. Plans for the Advent-Christmas-Epiphany cycle could be developed during the fall of the year, those for the Easter cycle during January, for the summer portion of Pentecost during the month of May, and for the last half of Pentecost during July or August.

Preachers who develop such a preaching plan avoid the pitfalls of the "homiletical crash program" that calls for the sermon to be crafted completely in a few days of the week. They almost never come up "dry." They have the opportunity to accumulate preaching materials — stories and illustrations, to react to movies and drama and TV — instead of attempting to find such sermonic items at the last minute. They might discover that they not only have time to prepare properly on paper, but to learn the sermon for delivery, too. They may learn that the Word can come alive in their preaching as never before when this sort of system is in their preaching ministry. A short-term — within the week — preaching plan is essential, but for excellence in preaching a long-term plan is indispensable. The church year offers such a plan — *the Story* — to conscientious preachers.

A Church-Year Sermon in Narrative Form

The church year calls attention to a story, the Story of God's gift to the world, Jesus Christ. By its very nature, it encourages God's preachers to tell that Story to their people, yet it imposes no single narrative shape upon the sermon. One thing that the preacher has to keep in mind as he or she attempts to prepare and tell the Story is how that pericope-story speaks to people today and meets the needs of persons living right now.

There will always be different, yet biblical, ways to tell the Story.

About a decade ago, when the use of story in the pulpit was being encouraged and attempted, Oswald Hoffman preached a radio sermon titled "Born Free." The text is part of the John 8 pericope appointed for the Festival of the Reformation: "If the Son shall make you free, you will be free indeed." The sermon is textual yet expository, topical yet narrative in style, interweaving the text and its theme with a contemporary story and the people's stories in the sermon. Informed by the kerygma and sound theology, it is also thoroughly evangelical. I see it as an excellent example of how to make a single verse into a narrative sermon by combining a contemporary story with it. Perhaps Dr. Hoffman had been thinking about the text when he was reading the story about Jonathan Livingston Seagull, and then and there the sermon idea was born — or it could have been developed some other way. At any rate, it is worth reading and studying — and analyzing — as a sermon shape for preparing story sermons on epistle texts as well as the gospel stories.

"Born Free"
Oswald Hoffmann

Most gulls don't bother to learn more than the simplest facts of flight — how to get from shore to food and back again. For most gulls, it is not flying that matters, but eating. For this gull, though, it was not eating that mattered, but flight. More than anything else, Jonathan Livingston Seagull loved to fly.

That's from a best seller in the United States titled simply *Jonathan Livingston Seagull, A Story,* by Richard Bach, with magnificent photographs of seagulls in flight by Richard Munson.

Jonathan Livingston Seagull is a kind of parable. It describes the adventures of a gull who broke through the usual customs of the flock, soaring to extraordinary heights and speeds, breaking through even the usual restrictions of space and time.

I have talked to a lot of people who have read this story, this parable, and each one saw in it something different. Some immediately talked about Jonathan Livingston Seagull as if he were human. Others treated it for what it is: a story about a seagull. Still others saw in it overtones of various kinds, a commentary on all of life.

The theme of the story is how one gull found freedom, and then shared it with others who didn't think such freedom was possible. Indeed, the one gull was ostracized by the flock because he broke out of the usual way of doing things.

The whole thing is a fantasy, of course, and fantasies don't have to be justified except to those who cannot accept the fact that it is a fantasy. This one can't be justified on a lot of grounds. It refuses to recognize that gulls have certain limitations, but that's the story.

When Jonathan Seagull joined the flock on the beach, it was full night. He was dizzy and terribly tired. Yet in delight he flew a loop to landing, with a snap roll just before touchdown. When they hear of it, he thought, of the Breakthrough, they'll be wild with joy. How much more there is now to living! Instead of our drab slogging back and forth to the fishing, there's a reason to life! We can lift ourselves out of ignorance, we can find ourselves as creatures of excellence and intelligence and skill. We can be free! We can learn to fly!

That reminds me of something our Lord said to human beings; to people, not to seagulls: "If the Son shall make you free, you will be free indeed." Preposterous as it may sound to a lot of people, he meant exactly what he said. It is possible for people to be free, amid all the limitations of life, with a clean breakthrough that comes in a remarkable way by direct, straightforward faith in Jesus Christ.

He himself talked in parables. He said if you have faith as a grain of mustard seed, you might say to this sycamine tree, "be plucked up by the root and be planted in the midst of the sea, and it would obey you." That's pretty strong talk, but not too strong for him, and not too strong for people who are willing to try it. Faith has power, indescribable power, when it is faith in him.

The flight of birds has always been impressive to people. With all the dangers of life attached to birds, flight has the charm of breaking away from earth, and maybe, from the earthy. The first attempts of human beings to fly, from Icarus to the modern age, were efforts to copy the flight of birds, with flapping wings and even feathers. When people actually did learn to fly, they used the principles of aerodynamics which govern the flight of birds.

The Bible is full of references to birds. "Birds shall tell the matter" said the writer of Ecclesiastes. Hosea talked about flying away like a bird. Jeremiah spoke of making one's nest high as that of an eagle. Obadiah talked about setting his nest on the stars. Describing himself, our Lord said, "Birds have nests and the foxes have holes, but the Son of Man has nowhere to lay His head." People understand that kind of language. Having a mortgage is not everything, but he did not even have that.

In many respects, Jonathan Livingston Seagull was an ordinary bird. He looked like the other seagulls. In other respects, he was not ordinary. As it turned out, he reached speeds and heights which were thought to be forbidden to seagulls. He survived death, and he came back from the dead. He defied angry mobs of jealous seagulls and left a trail of disciples behind to carry out his mission. Rejected by his flock as an outcast, he learned the secret of flight. His instructor, an older gull named Chiang, explained the secret of flight. "The trick," according to Chiang, was for Jonathan to stop seeing himself as trapped inside a limited body that had a forty-two-inch wingspan and performance that could be plotted on a chart. The trick was to know that his true nature lived, as perfect as an unwritten number, everywhere at once across space and time.

The key to achieving this perfect state, as the fantasy goes, is understanding. If only Jonathan could understand his true nature, he would be able to get outside himself.

It is a liberating thought. I imagine that is why the story appeals to so many people, and why it has turned out to be a best seller. People like to hear that kind of stuff. If only they could get outside themselves! If only they could learn the secret of life! If only somebody would discover the secret and share it with the rest of us!

People are looking for hope in a world that has lost hope. It is not only Jonathan who wants to fly higher and faster than he's supposed to. Humankind feels that there is more to life than what it is getting. Despite the wars, the greed, the hatred, the jealousy, and the anger, our world has a sneaking hunch that people were put on earth for more than this. If only we knew what it is, and then if we could find it and have it!

Jonathan Livingston Seagull seems to say to people today, "The key to my own flight, and to the soaring of humanity lies in self-understanding, grasping the powers in the heart of man, and then holding fast to that knowledge despite opposition."

Some people like to think of Jesus Christ as one of those special people who have found a special secret — a sort of key to all of life. If you can get that secret, they seem to think, you will have the key, and you will be free. Jonathan Livingston Seagull is a fantasy, and so is this a fantasy, that Jesus Christ is just a discoverer of some secret. Far from breaking through the bounds of space and time, he took all of that for himself. The Son of God became a man, not the other way around. The story of Christmas and of Calvary is not of a man finding out how to be God but of God becoming a man, becoming a part of history and taking everything that goes with that.

It is not a question of man realizing his possibilities, but of God taking man as he is, doing for him what he cannot do for himself, atoning for his sins, and bringing him back again to what he can be without carrying a load of guilt upon his back. Forgiveness from God is liberating, and that's in Jesus Christ. Forgiveness frees a man to be a man today and tomorrow, as no man can be without that forgiveness from God, and as no man will be without wholehearted acceptance of that forgiveness from God himself. That's what it takes to be a man and to be free. "If the Son shall make you free, you will be free indeed."

Appealing as it may be to the instincts of man for freedom, Jonathan's philosophy is quite different. "They are saying in the flock that if you are the son of the great gull himself," Fletcher told Jonathan one morning after advanced speed practice, "that you are a thousand years ahead of your time." Jonathan sighed. The price of being misunderstood, he thought. They call you a devil or they call you God. "What do you think, Fletch? Are we ahead of our time?" A long silence. "Well, this kind of flying has always been here to be learned by anybody who wanted to discover it; that's got nothing to do with time. We are ahead of the fashion, maybe. Ahead of the way that most gulls fly."

That's appealing to people. They like to think that somehow they can do it their own way, get ahead of the game. Jonathan's sign of hope, salvation "from within" is appealing to people. It gives them a picture of perfection that can be achieved by working hard enough at it. Given enough time, enough patience, you can arrive.

It all depends on the teachers, of course; the enlightened ones who can show us the way. Then, like a downhill snowball, we'll gain momentum. We can get outside ourselves. We can overcome sin, we can beat greed, we can stamp out ghettos and prisons and POW camps all by ourselves. Give us enough time and resources, and freedom will happen.

Appealing as it is, that's a dead-end street. I am sorry to have to tell you that, but it doesn't work. It's been tried, and it hasn't worked. Here it is again, in a really beautiful story about a seagull. When you are finished with it, you know it won't work, but it is a beautiful dream, isn't it?

I am not talking about a dream, today. I am talking about what is real. "If the Son shall make you free, you will be free indeed." This is not a preacher talking. This is the Son of God himself, the One who died and was raised from the dead to be declared the Son of God with power. He has got it, including the resurrection and everything. He has got the whole world in his hands, because he is Lord. He has got it to give, and he gives it. "If the Son makes you free, you will be free indeed."

I know that doesn't seem possible in our workaday world. We have tried our wings. We have soared to certain heights, we have raced with the speed of sound and beyond. What it really takes, however, we lack. All of us know that Jonathan Livingston Seagull makes for great reading — and dreaming — but its vision is hollow.

*Vanity of vanity, futility of futilities, said the
preacher, all is vanity, all is futility. What does a
man gain by all the toil at which he toils under
the sun? A generation goes and a generation
comes but the earth remains forever. What has
been is what will be, and what has been done is
what will be done; there is nothing new under the
sun.* (Ecclesiastes 1:2, 3, 9)

That's man as he is. As people say, "That's us, as we
are." That's the picture of man we see on the television
screen, every day on the front pages of newspapers and
in the history books. It faces us in the quiet moments of
our solitude when we look at the real self that only we
know.

There is another preacher. St. Paul was not talking
about seagulls but about people, about himself, telling it
like it is: "For I know that nothing good dwells within
me, that is, in my flesh. I can will what is right, but I
cannot do it. I do not do the good I want, but the evil I
do not want is what I do . . . Wretched man that I am!
Who will deliver me from this body of death?"

Jonathan might say, if you take this fantasy about
seagulls as having something to say to people, "Reach
beyond that, grab hold of the real — the real you behind
this self-condemning front of yours. That's the way to
fly, Paul!"

Paul knew something that Jonathan doesn't. He is
just a seagull, after all. The best of men, trying to fly by
convincing themselves of their own godliness, have only
deceived themselves. That kind of life is hypocrisy. Paul
had to see himself as he was, rebel, runaway, afraid to
face up to his own identity. Only by fully confronting
the evil that is in man's heart can that man stand wide
open to the grace of God that comes to those who are
poor in spirit.

The fantasy of Jonathan Seagull does not end with

flight. He goes on to discover the secret of life: Truth, love, understanding, unlimited capabilities lie within your own head and heart. You like that? A lot of people do. I wish it were true, but it isn't. All of us know better. It may sound all right to a seagull, but it's pretty frothy when it comes to people.

Jonathan learned to do full wing snap rolls, barrel loops, and 135 to 234 miles an hour. Through that, he came to know the secret of life, that truth, goodness, and beauty are the real thing. That sounds awfully good. Then the other gulls began to refer to him as the son of the great gull, a thousand years ahead of his time.

That's Jonathan. The Son of God is not named Jonathan. His name is Jesus. He, too, gave of himself and he had to take opposition from the flock. But that's where the similarity ends. Jonathan strained and stretched, tucked in his wings and soared to new heights in a fit of glee. Jesus, Son of the Almighty God, humbled himself and became obedient unto death, even the death of the cross. That's no way to fly. It isn't excitement, but it is agony. No thrill of pulling out of a dive at 193 miles per hour; only seven hours between two thieves on a scaffold put up by the executioners!

The breathtaking surprise is that all of this happened for us. It wasn't the unfortunate end of a bumbling prophet. It was God's plan that his Son should die in order that his flock, his disobedient flock, might come back again as part of the family.

God doesn't show us how we can do it ourselves. He sent Jesus Christ to be the Savior of the world. Jesus is not a teacher to unlock certain secrets in our heads and set us sailing to new heights of awareness. His way is sacrifice, and that's a real one, for freedom.

"If the Son shall make you free, you will be free indeed." That comes from God who gave up His Son for us all. It comes to those who are, so to speak, reborn for freedom. As one of his men said, "For freedom

Christ has made you free."

Talk about being born free, this is it! We are too far gone to cash in on our birth. We have to be reborn to freedom. That rebirth is by faith in Jesus Christ, crucified and resurrected Son of God.

Accept the invitation of Jesus, follow him, and discover how fresh and exhilarating life can be with him. With Jesus Christ, life has purpose and meaning. With Jesus Christ you have a direction to travel and power to go that way. It's a little like flying, and the motive power comes from his Spirit.

Jonathan was right about one thing. He diagnosed the situation very well. "The reason a gull can't fly as high and as fast as his capabilities allow is fear — fear of the unknown, of failure and defeat." A lot of people are the same way. They won't take the risk of faith in Christ, because they are afraid to do it. That's the only way. Faith in Christ, with his forgiveness and his life that he shares with those who trust in him, carried ordinary people past the terrors of the unknown, the fear of death and the terrible haunting fear of guilt around which so many people are trying to walk all the time. Faith just carried through when it is faith in Christ.

St. Paul, whose life was filled with failure and defeat, persecution and frustration, was talking about something real when he said, "I can do all things through Jesus Christ who strengthens me." Now, that's audacity, a little bit like that of a little seagull named Jonathan. There is one big difference. In Jesus Christ the dream of freedom and of flight comes true. It is like being reborn. That is the way to fly. It is the way to go. Amen.*

_____

*"Born Free" by Oswald Hoffmann. Used by permission of the International Lutheran Laymen's Leaque, sponsor of "The Lutheran Hour."

3 Preaching Within the Liturgy

During the past two decades, some homileticians were asking a question about the role of preaching in worship: "Where shall we place the pulpit?"[1] Liturgical experts during the same period were asking, "Where should the altar be located in the nave?" And, "What kind of altar should church buildings have today in the light of a changing liturgy?" In many churches, the altar is a simple table, free-standing but located variously in the worship space. In some buildings, such as St. Stephen Lutheran Church in Williamsburg, Virginia — a "contemporary-colonial" and octagonal church built on a plan created by Thomas Jefferson for a church never built in his day — the table is central and the people are seated almost all of the way around it. In other churches, the altar-table is placed in front of the pews or chairs. The question of where to place the altar has not been fully resolved, but there is considerable ecumenical agreement that it should be in the form of a table — the "Table of the Lord."

The question of locating — or relocating — the pulpit has not yet been settled. Some are in the corners of contemporary structures, some in front of the table, others behind the table, a few are attached to the table and loom above it, and some are by the side of it. At least one liturgically-informed architect argues that the altar-table and the pulpit should be side by side, balanced, as it were, in the front of the nave so that people could see — and comprehend — the relationship of the Word and the Sacrament of the Altar. And not a few buildings have grouped together the table, the pulpit, and the font as testimony to the ways that God comes to his people in Jesus Christ. Preachers, planning committees, and architects still seem to be at odds as to where the pulpit should be placed in the church. Pulpits, practically, seem to be almost "free-floating" rather than free-standing like so many altar-tables in contemporary use.

In *The Church Incarnate,* Rudolph Schwarz rendered a service to people concerned about the arrangement of furniture in the church, one that was quite similar to Adrian Nocent's contribution to liturgiologists in his *The Future of the Liturgy.* He went back to the early church and identified four floor plans which, as they were developed, revealed the ecclesiology of the people who constructed the buildings. Each plan indicated the liturgical posture of the pastor-bishop and the people — the clergy and the laity. One, in which the pastor stands/sits before the people, pictures him/her as pastor of the flock, the person who gathers the people before the table of the Lord and tells them the stories of the faith that make sense of history and life and give meaning to their journey. He or she is also at the head of the procession of God's people in their pilgrimage through the world toward the fulfillment God has promised in the age to come. The relationship of pastor and people in worship, plus the pastor's function as preacher/presider, ought to be the determining factor in the placement of pulpit. altar, and the seats for the people. Since pulpits, particularly, are found in a variety of locations in church naves, it is obvious that the question, "Where shall we place the pulpit (and the altar, too, to a lesser degree) in the church?" has not, as yet, been answered to everyone's satisfaction.

Preaching Within Liturgical Worship

A quarter of a century ago, Reginald Fuller asked a question that is related to the pulpit-table question — and could settle it for most liturgical churches. The title of his little classic is *What Is Liturgical Preaching?* As worship and preaching were experiencing changes in the 1960s and 1970s, others have addressed the same question[2] which Fuller raised in 1958. Liturgical preaching is being taken more seriously by greater numbers of scholars and preachers. Liturgiologists and homileticians are engaged in discussions about the relationship of worship and preaching; their professional societies have met together to share papers, discussion, and worship. Liturgical preaching is receiving more attention than it ever has before,[3] and considerable progress has been made in answering Fuller's query in the light of new liturgies and new lectionaries in the churches. In the excellent little book, *Word and Table,* produced by the United Methodist Church to encourage and assist in the use of *The Sacrament of the Lord's Supper: An Alternate Text 1972,* the worship committee of the Board of Discipleship writes: "The restoration of the unified liturgy of the early churches, consisting of the reading of Scripture and proclamation, congregational prayer, praise and response, and the sacramental sign-actions of bread and wine, brings . . . new theological understandings (about preaching and worship)."[4] Fuller asked a theological question — not one related to ritual or ceremony — that demands theological consideration and response in all churches and from all preachers who take liturgy seriously.

The basic characteristics, or marks, of liturgical preaching were quite well established before the publication of new worship books and related materials. These are four in number:

1. Liturgical preaching is *worship-related*; it is done within the worship service. The *setting is liturgical, not homiletical,* despite the centrality of the Word — read and preached — in the Sunday (eucharistic) service.

2. Liturgical preaching is *biblical.* As *Word and Table* aptly says it: "The sermon is part of the proclaiming and hearing of the Scriptures, thus emphasizing preaching as a contemporary witness to the Word."[5]

3. Liturgical preaching is *kerygmatic* in that its perspective, through the church year, is from God's redeeming events in Christ — death, resurrection, and the parousia.

4. Liturgical preaching is *sacramentally-oriented* — to the Sacrament of Baptism as well as the Eucharist. On Sundays, a service in which the Word is preached without Holy Communion is incomplete, a "half-mass" or "torso" as some have termed it.

As the new liturgies and lectionaries began to make their appearance, a fifth mark has been identified, as David Babin and others interested in the relationship of worship and preaching have noted: The sermon "is an integral part of the liturgy" and, Babin insists, "performs a liturgical function."[6] When he discusses "The Sermon as Part of the Liturgy,"[7] as Paul Bosch would address this relationship, Fr. Gerard Sloyan includes the functional role of sermon in liturgy, too: "It is always in order for the homilist to draw the worshiper into the action of the praise of God by Christ, in the Spirit, which the worshiper is shortly to do sacramentally in his role as priest."[8] The preaching of the Word within the Sunday liturgy, therefore, is intended to stir up a response to the Word so that they may go to the altar-table singing their song of praise and thanksgiving to the Lord, their God.

The Message of Liturgical Preaching

Genuine Christian preaching always is, and will be, the proclamation of God's activity in this world in Jesus Christ. "Preaching proclaims a message," declares Richard R. Caemmerer.

> *The message is from God. God wants to tell me about the life which he has for them as a gift . . . Preaching tells of God's gift of life, which he gives to men through His Son, Jesus Christ, who died on the Cross and rose again that men might live.*[9]

It was the death and resurrection of the One who "became obedient unto death" that initiated the most startling — and the best — news that humanity has ever heard. That message, repeated over and over for two thousand years, is the heart of the gospel; it is always fresh because it is addressed to people who have been — or are — estranged from God and have no hope.

With its emphasis placed upon Sunday as the "little Easter," liturgical preaching underlines the resurrection of Jesus Christ — and death and resurrection are considered to be a unitive event in this respect — in the church's celebration. "Christian preaching was born in the resurrection of Jesus,'' says Richard Lischer.

It happened this way: one disciple, trembling, cried out in a breaking, terrified voice, 'Christ is risen!' and the receiver of the message made it a sermon by completing the circuit and exulting, 'He is risen indeed!' . . . It was the resurrection that validated Jesus' ministry, his announcement of the Kingdom, his ethical teachings, and finally his death.

Lischer seems almost to echo Gustav Wingren's exhortation (in *The Living Word*) when he writes: "Let the reminder for preachers be: only because of the resurrection does Christian preaching assume the significance and importance so desperately claimed for it."[10] It is not surprising that Lischer joins the ranks of those who have insisted that the kerygma is the heart of liturgical preaching.[11] And he is right when he concludes: "Fifty-one Sundays of the year, only dimly do preachers remember this fountain of all preaching."[12] Liturgical preaching is and has to be kerygmatic, occurring as it does in a kerygmatic setting — "little Easter" — every week as the faithful followers of Christ gather in his name.

The preacher's task is to proclaim that message in such a way that it becomes a current event in the experience of God's people in this time and place, so that whenever the gospel — "He is risen!" — is announced, people might respond with certainty and joy, "He is risen indeed!" — now! H. Grady Davis suggested that contemporaneity in preaching the gospel is achieved, in part, by preparing and speaking the sermon in the present tense and the indicative mood.[13] Gerard Sloyan affirms this when he discusses liturgical preaching and offers a kind of formula to preachers to assist them in grounding the gospel in life today:

1. The homily (or sermon) is spoken prose in a particular life situation; it has no proper existence apart from this situation, and in the medium of speech.

2. The homily attempts to situate the hearer in his own life through the Bible, and not in the life of the men of the Bible.[14]

The tense and mood of the sermon are one of the means — but not the only one — by which preachers may accomplish this.

Liturgical preaching of the gospel message begins with a *dual perspective*, the Christ-event (death and resurrection) as the source of the Christian oral communication *and* the weekly gathering of the Christian community for the worship and praise of God. The gospel must be preached to these faithful people who come together to celebrate Jesus' resurrection but who desperately need to be renewed through the Word and the Spirit. They have experienced the healing power of the gospel, but they have been wounded by life; they have known reconciliation with God and each other but have been separated once more by sin; they have everything in Christ but need the very power of God to deal with life in hope and on a day-to-day basis. Bishop James Armstrong, in *Telling Truth,*[15] doesn't believe that all gospel preaching does this, and he states that "much preaching is unrelated to forms of reality most people are called upon to cope with." A *dual perspective* — the gospel of the suffering, dying, risen and reigning Christ over against and proclaimed to the real people who make up the body of believers at worship today — is a first step in making the sermon a relevant and contemporary message for this last part of the twentieth century. Under this pressure, the perspective of liturgical preaching takes on a sixth characteristic: it becomes *pastoral proclamation* of the gospel.

The Sunday assembly of the people of the parish gives the pastor the best opportunity of the week to be pastor to most of the people he serves. Regardless of the amount of counseling he or she may do, the contacts he/she makes with people in meetings and in the work of the parish, his or her home and hospital visits, and all other ways that pastoral communication takes place, on Sunday, he/she ministers — through the Word — to more people at one time than in all of these combined. That's why Domenico Grasso says that the proclamation of the Word "is the most important thing the priest does in the mass," adding, "In preaching the Word is addressed to all who have assembled."[16] And, in his opinion, that's why it is also the most difficult that the preacher undertakes; the Word has to be preached so that it becomes personal and vital to all those hearing the sermon. Pastoral proclamation of the gospel is esential in Sunday preaching.

Edification — the Function of Liturgical Preaching

In the introductions to his useful four-volume series, *The Sermon and the Propers*, Fred H. Lindemann [17] gave an exhaustive list of the functions that preaching might perform in the liturgy. H. Grady Davis's list of "functional forms" was, on the other hand, limited to three: proclamation, teaching, and therapy. Arndt Halvorson writes, "There are only two reasons for preaching. One is conversion; the other is upbuilding." And in his theology of preaching, *Proclaiming God's Message,* Professor Grasso returns to three functions: missionary preaching, catechization, and liturgical preaching; he excludes the first two from normal Sunday — eucharistic — preaching, and, too, believes, that liturgical preaching should edify and build up mature Christians in the faith. While Halvorson sees conversion as "the shifting of allegiance," Grasso envisions the preaching of the gospel as more of a "call back to allegiance to Christ" which, for him, requires the preaching of the law as well as the gospel. Halvorson might be speaking for both when he says:

> *In either case we preach in the hope that we can help the breakthrough to the life of faith. There is not so much difference between conversion and upbuilding. Each is characterized by an experience — seeing things in a new light, a new relativity of ideas and focus, new possibilities. Each happens through the elusive, yet always persuasive, quality we know as insight. When people are converted they say to themselves, "I am persuaded," "I am convinced," "I believe," "I trust." When people experience Christian growth they often say, "I see." "I see my sin," or ". . . my foolishness," or ". . . how he has been answering my prayers," or ". . . my neighbor," or ". . . how I must rely more solidly on his grace."* [18]

And, again, he reminds preachers: "We must never lose sight of the delicate manner in which grace breaks through."

Pastoral preaching must also have an eschatological dimension to it that assures people that God's plan to initiate the fulness of the Kingdom in the future — through Christ — will be realized. God's will cannot be thwarted by the designs of a sinful and recalcitrant humanity, as our Lord prayed, "Thy will be done, thy kingdom come, on earth as it is in heaven." How and when God will usher in the "reign of peace" with its justice and mercy for all people will remain a mystery until it happens. But it will occur — and that's the difference between his Story and many of our stories. Through the gospel as it is preached, that is what gives people hope "when there is no hope."

Pastoral preaching is theological preaching of the appointed scriptural selections — and in the context of the gospel — in sermons that are in the present tense, indicative mood, as in the telling of a story. Thus, Arndt Halvorson asks a rhetorical question of preachers: "Can we even do theology (in sermons) without the help of the story form and the involvement of people who are wrestling with the questions addressed by the theologian (pastor)?"[19] Story offers a methodology and form to engage in the preaching of theologically-loaded sermons for the upbuilding and edification of God's people, especially as it is grounded in baptismal and Eucharistic preaching.

Until recently, baptismal preaching has been overlooked by most preachers, probably because the sacrament of Holy Communion tends to overshadow it. Communion sermons find a place in most preachers' sermonic output, sometimes as often as once a month. Their content has to do with repentance, forgiveness, the restoration of people to their God through the death and resurrection of Christ. The Eucharist renews — again and again — what has been given in Holy Baptism.

Baptismal preaching is rich theologically and, too, as story. It takes Donald Capps' theological motifs for preaching (the will of God, human responsibility and initiative, the grace of God, hope in God, truth in our relation to God, and the communal dimensions of our relation to God) and ties them into the lives of believers. Baptism not only is an initiatory rite that establishes our relationship with Christ and the Church, it also spells out our response — daily repentance and renewal — and our responsibilities (love, service, evangelism, care of the poor, peacemaking, etc.) in the world. It is best done as story preaching. See my *You Are My Beloved Children* [Concordia] and *Plastic Flowers in the Holy Water* [C.S.S.] for examples of such preaching during the Easter cycle.)

Liturgical Preaching and Pastoral Exegesis

Liturgical preaching depends upon a two-phase process for developing a biblical text into a sermon. Biblical exegesis is the first and fundamental step in the process and much has been written about that. In an article, "Preparing the Homily,"[20] Reginald Fuller offers a compact method for doing biblical exegesis: translation or reading of the text in at least two different translations, reconstruction of the situation for which the text was originated by employing the tools for critical study of the Bible to determine what the text meant — and means — today, culminating in a paraphrase of the text. Exposition emerges when pastoral reflection, or exegesis (called *Predigtmeditation* by the Germans), engages the pastor:

> *The pastor has to concern himself with two poles — the original message of the pericope, as distilled from the exegesis* [and] *the current situation of his audience or congregation as he envisages it when they are gathered for the liturgy. Here he will have to draw upon his knowledge of their concerns (as he has experienced or perceived them in his pastoral relationship to them)* . . .[21]

The combination of pastoral care and perception makes it possible for him or her to bridge the gap between exegesis and exposition, the Bible story and the people, and to arrive at a message for this occasion. The task, at that point, is to formulate it into a sermon that will make sense to them and edify them.

In the process of the reflection that takes place after the exegesis, theology comes into play. Fuller explains:

> *Then he will decide how the text speaks in judgment and memory, in wrath and grace to this situation. He must ask: What is the law and what is the gospel in the text? Finally, he should envisage the result he looks for from his hearers: repentance, renewed faith, some act of devotion or some concrete act of obedience.*[22]

Only then is the pastor ready to shape the message into a sermon that will communicate the gospel to the congregation.

The Role of Perception in Pastoral Preaching

Liturgical preaching utilizes perception in pastoral exegesis and preaching to determine the signs of the times in which people and pastors live and to shape effective and existential sermons from the Word. Perception provides insight into the human dilemma in the world and uncovers the common ground of that experience so that people and preacher might meet — through the Word — in the preaching event. It is critical to the process of reflection on the Word and the human situation to be addressed.

In the first chapter of *Wind, Sand and Stars,* entitled "The Craft," Antoine de St. Exupery might have been discussing the pastoral role of the preacher, instead of an airmail pilot, when he describes how he got ready for his first flight. He had gone to see his friend Guillamet, who taught him how to do the exegesis of the flight by probing the mysteries of the terrain of Spain and the Pyrenees. Of that experience, he wrote:

*Little by little, under the lamp, the Spain of my
map became a sort of fairyland. The crosses I
marked to indicate safety zones and traps were
so many buoys and beacons. I charted the
farmer, the thirty sheep, the brook. And exactly
where she stood, I set a buoy to mark the shep-
herdess forgotten by the geographers.*

After that meeting, which Antoine called a "strange
lesson in geography," he remarked, "Guillamet did not
teach Spain to me, he made the country my friend."
That suggests to me what ought to happen in biblical
exegesis as the foundation of sermon preparation.
"Mastery of the text" — in this case, the map of Spain
— was essential to undertaking the task of an airmail
pilot in the 1930s.

After leaving Guillamet, Antoine — for *Wind, Sand
and Stars* is an autobiographical account of part of his
life as a pilot and a reporter — walked through the city
on "a freezing winter night" which he later describes:

*I turned up my coat collar, and as I strode among
the indifferent passersby I was escorting a fervor
as tender as if I had just fallen in love . . . These
passersby knew nothing about me, (but) they
were about to confide the weightiest cares of
their hearts and their trade (to me). Into my
hands were they about to entrust their hopes.
And I, muffled up in my cloak, walked among
them like a shepherd.*

Again, with the perception of the pastor facing the task
of preparing and preaching a sermon to his or her
parish, Antoine reflects:

*Nor were they receiving any of those messages
now being dispatched to me by the night. For this*

snowstorm that was gathering, and that was to burden my first flight concerned my frail flesh, not theirs . . . My footfall rang in a universe that was not theirs.

Doesn't that sound like the lonely and difficult task that the preacher faces each week as he wrestles with a pericope and attempts to shape the lesson(s) into a meaningful message from God for the people? And Antoine understood, as a pastor should, the world of the people he saw that night:

These messages of such grave concern were reaching me as I walked between rows of lighted show windows, and those windows on that night seemed a display of all that was good on earth, or a paradise of sweet things . . . What meaning could they have for me, these lamps whose glow was to shelter men's meditations, those cozy furs out of which were to emerge pathetically beautiful, solicitous faces? I was still wrapped in the aura of friendship, expectant of surprise and palpitatingly prepared for happiness; and yet already I was soaked in spray; a mail pilot, I was already nibbling the bitter pulp of night flight.[23]

The business of preaching the Word is like that. The preacher needs to develop the kind of sensitivity toward people — as well as the Word — that is requisite in the preacher. Preaching, in the opinion of Paul Harms, is "more perception than conception." The preacher has to learn to see — for that's what perception is — before he or she can preach effectively to people. In his book about preaching and perception, Clement Welsh says, "Preaching is a pastoral action. Like pastoral counseling, it is intended to help the person discover the gospel for himself, and to make it his own . . ." The preacher, therefore, must "see" the universe in biblical and human perspective: "To make sense of a world one must observe it, and not as an undifferentiated blur but as a collection of entities that are identifiable, and take their place in relationships that can be plotted and organized."[24]

Welsh believes that perception is indispensable not only in arriving at a message to the people but also in the actual construction of the sermon. Perception helps the preacher to choose language that will make people think, quicken their imaginations, and involve them in the preaching event. Too often, language does not do this:

> *A Sunday service with sermon can constitute a brief moment with God-talk but often the discussion at the coffee hour afterward reveals how much deep confusion has not been dealt with. The institutional results are predictable — a strong and growing biblical fundamentalism, immersed in a religion of the past; a fringe group of experimentalists, searching for renewal within the life of the emotions; and a middle group that continues on by habit, finding little that speaks to their condition, and which drifts away bodily and mentally.*[25]

Perception will not only change language, but also excites the imagination of the preacher which might change the shape of the sermon. It urges more use of extended imagery, especially illustration that is in the form of story — not merely to gain the interest of the hearers but to get them involved imaginatively with the Word that is being preached. Pastors attempting to communicate theologically *and* imaginatively, thereby avoiding the dullness that seems to be built into much biblical preaching, ought to study the word of Loren

Eiseley. Professor James Mays once said that every theological student and pastor should know Eiseley's writings; he interprets science through story in a manner that suggests how pastors might preach biblical theology with imagination through story — the Story — to their people. We will reserve further study of Loren Eiseley's work for a later chapter in this book. For now, it is enough to state that pastoral perception enables the preacher to see into and beyond the obvious mysteries of life in this world and enables the preacher to discover that imaginative language, especially in story form, will alter the shape of the sermon so as to invite people to participate in the sermon event in the hope of finding new and surprising encounters with the Word, Jesus Christ.

A Story Sermon that Integrates Literature and the Bible

Charles Rice, one of the three main collaborators in the conception and writing of *Preaching the Story,* makes extensive use of narrative in his sermons. He writes that:

> *Continued experience in the work of preaching has led me to think that the preacher's vocation is translation, the apt and artful presentation of the gospel in contemporary idiom. The saving grace of Christian communication today is imagination, that habit of mind which can move from one's own situation into a new frame of reference, enriching both "worlds" by the very movement.*

A seminar on doctrinal preaching when he was a doctoral student at Union Theological Seminary, New York, forced him to face the question, "How does one preach on the cardinal doctrines without resorting to time-honored theological language?'' He was also taking a course on "Christian Faith and Modern Fiction," and he says, "The possibility of preaching within a new frame of reference, the world of literature, only gradually came into view."[26] The combination of those two sermons resulted in a sermon inspired by William Faulkner's *The Sound and the Fury* that "remains for me the most satisfactory expression of the meaning of the doctrine of the second coming of Christ."

Some of Charles Rice's sermons could be called expository in that he retells a story, comments upon it, weaves in — at times — the biblical story, or text, and creates interesting and involving sermons. As in many story sermons, the text might be oblique, the message intriguing but abstract from the viewpoint of the biblical text. The reader will make judgments on his or her own about the content and the shape of the sermon which follows and integrates the doctrine of the second coming — and three biblical texts — with Faulkner's novel. Exposition of the Revelation texts is also done in story-form within the sermon and the story from literature. It might be used as an occasional shape for variety. The sermon also demonstrates the role of perception in pastoral preaching as he weaves together the biblical texts, *The Sound and the Fury,* and "Gabriel" on top of Riverside Church, into a message on Christ's second coming.

"The First and the Last"
Charles L. Rice

Lessons: Psalm 90; Revelation 1:7-11, 21:1-6

We meet the Compsons during Holy Week.

Their story unfolds against a backdrop of suffering and death.

But perhaps we should not speak of their *story,* for these people do not move through time as story does.

They are suspended in meaninglessness; unable to fulfill the time, they try either to fill it up or to escape.

Quentin Compson, frustrated by forbidden incestuous longing, tears the hands from the clock and jumps to his death in the Charles River.

Jason, who measures time by money hoarded, has no compassionate time for anyone, and in the end has neither money nor love.

Young Miss Quentin, with no one to help make sense of her past, finds each day as aimless as it is frantic with passion.

We know them all:

Quentin who sees his life merely passing, going nowhere.

Jason, who tries to number his days by his bank-book, to give substance to life by acquisition.

Miss Quentin, drifting in lonely fantasy.

It seems that Benjy, the feebleminded one, is the most fortunate: better to have no sense of time than a life which is no more than one petty thing after another.

But what is the alternative?

How do we make sense of the passing of our days?

Can we fulfill time rather than merely filling it up?

Does the church make any sense at all when, hard up against the question, it affirms the second coming of Jesus Christ?

William Faulkner's answer is elusive, and we cannot know it until we have met Dilsey.

The novel, moving toward that meeting, is well named: it is just when life seems, as it does in the Compson household, a tale told by an idiot, that we are most open to visions of the Lord coming again among his people.

In short, John on Patmos, a young man alone in a big city, Dilsey in the Compson kitchen — they are at the place for speaking to the Compsons and to us about the advent of the Lord.

John of Patmos scanned the clouds, and understandably so. Jerusalem lay plundered, Rome was a-building, and John was stranded on the very island from which the Caesars quarried stone for their eternal city on the Tiber.

But John did not languish, nor did he wring his hands over what the world was coming to.

In the past, and present, was an event which would not allow him to take the measure of the world by Rome's impressive blocks of stone.

He laid his right hand upon me, saying, "Fear not, I am the first and the last, the living one; I died, and behold I am alive forevermore, and I have the keys of death and Hades." (Revelation 1:18)

John was as sure of the Omega as of the Alpha.

The Revelation of John is testimony to that faith, as dauntless as it is difficult to articulate, the faith of all those who in mourning over the world have waited for God's comfort.

For John it was the clouds and a new Jerusalem.

Paul had waited till the trumpet should sound and the Lord descend.

Hebrews has it simply, "Jesus Christ the same, yesterday, today, and forever."

But however it is put, it is the faith we share with John of Patmos, we who amid the very beauty of the autumn countryside remember that we, with our earthly city, are passing away.

We are likely listening for no trumpet.

The sound of one would conjure up Civil Defense, not Gabriel.

Nor do we turn our radar on the clouds in anticipation of a *friend.*

But we understand what John means.

Let us, therefore, celebrate our common faith in God's triumph.

John says that he shares three things with us:

I John your brother . . . share with you in Jesus the tribulation and the Kingdom and the patient endurance . . . (1:9)

In the midst of tribulation — and you can fill in what that means for you — we share the Kingdom.

We, like John, have seen the Kingdom of God, and consequently, we can no more be satisfied with the world than we can despair over it.

By the second coming of Jesus Christ we mean to say that in our past and present is a reality with ultimate implications.

Because we have heard the gospel, we listen for a trumpet.

The angel Gabriel stands on top of Riverside Church, his trumpet poised and his face lifted to the skies as if he were watching a jet take off from La-Guardia.

He is a parable in stone.

He stands firmly anchored to the stories past, surrounded by the bustling present, and obviously hopeful for the future.

His trumpet says that he has heard something, but his uplifted face says that he is looking for something out of sight.

His name means "man of God," herald of the Kingdom which is here and yet to come, at hand, around the corner, the city that is new, yet named Jerusalem.

For eight months I saw Gabriel every morning and night.

I went to work and play and worship, and he stood there all the while, his trumpet ready.

The foundations of the church on which he perches grab the bedrock of Manhattan as if intending to stand there by the Hudson forever.

And all the while Gabriel has his head in the clouds.

The stained glass round his feet points to the past, to faraway places and antique times.

Every Sunday Gabriel hears the same old story, told to people in well-worn pews, who expect to go to work on Monday and come back next Sunday.

They would be surprised to hear Gabriel toot his horn.

The days come and go, and Gabriel looks up into the sun and wind, sleet and snow.

He sees out of the corner of his eye that men still go down to the sea in ships, that the traffic becomes a little more hectic every Friday afternoon, and that the park turns russet autumn after autumn.

Summer and winter, seedtime and harvest, day and night, vary no more than the traffic lights.

But Gabriel keeps his horn ready.

And so it must be, that in the midst of our city we look for a city.

For the carillon plays and the people sing over and over: "Oh God our help in ages past, our hope for years to come . . ."

Our future rests firmly on our past.

Because stained glass points back to a stable and a cross and three travelers on Emmaus road, Gabriel can lift his trumpet.

It is what God has done that braces us for the living of these days, though we can do no better in charting our hope for the future than to use John's clouds and trumpets.

This hope, the hope of God's kingdom, enables us to live in the present and face the future as John did, in patient endurance, in that steadfastness founded in remembering and expecting, in that grace which sustains us at the Lord's table where we remember Jesus and wait in expectation.

The table is at once our confession that we cannot live our lives in the world by bread alone and our Thanksgiving that God nourishes his people.

And so we are able to endure, doing our work in the world, because all our expectations are in God.

Disappointment and disillusion are built into merely human hopes.

So we face a discouraging world as did John, with no confidence in the world, but in "the Lord, the everlasting God, the Creator of the ends of the earth, who does not faint or grow weary."

It is they who wait upon the Lord who shall renew their strength.

I cannot say how you are to wait, for I do not know what you must endure.

It is likely, however, that we will endure by doing our duty, that we will take the world seriously without taking it with utter seriousness, that we will live out this year, and succeeding years, but not merely as 1970 that year which is 1970 anno Domini.

We will go on doing our push-ups and pushing pencils and making pies.

We will go to the dentist twice a year and do our homework, and save for our children's future.

For to wait on the Lord as if the world were of no account is to miss the Kingdom which is in our midst.

To neglect human things is to deny the First Coming, the Incarnation by which God has hallowed earthly things and made our life all of a piece.

We wait not only in work, but in rest, for to know that the world passes away does not make us frantic to stay the days or to fear the future.

We know that the Word of our God stands, and so we pass our days in quietness and peace and at night go content to our beds.

We endure time as those who know that all our times are in his hands, past, present, and future.

But while we wait in work and rest, we mourn for the world.

The very fact that Gabriel is there is a symbol of our holy dissatisfaction.

Had John been content with things as they were, how would he have seen a new city?

But all is not well, no more than in the old Jerusalem over which Jesus mourned.

And we are never so much in his company, nor so near to the pathos of Gabriel's searching eye, as when we weep over the daily newspaper, over the life of the world.

"Blessed are they that mourn, for they shall be comforted."

But our weeping is not that of sentimentality or of despair, for that is not the mourning which is in itself blessedness.

It is the comforted grief of those who have seen and who wait to see the salvation of God.

For while we mourn over the world, we know the meaning of the promise, "Blessed are they that mourn . . ."

We endure patiently as those who know that the valleys will be exalted and the hills made low, even as in Israel's crooked time a voice was heard: "Comfort ye, comfort ye, my people."

Everyone of us has his own Patmos, and you will have to make John's vision your own, but the vision of faith makes possible our patient endurance.

Who knows this better than Dilsey, who does her duty in the world, knowing all the while that the world is coming to an end, the world where so much is wrong?

Dilsey is the old Negro servant, the mammy, in the Compson household, a family for whom life is all sound and fury, signifying nothing.

Dilsey is the only person in the family who will accept suffering, who will accept life as it is.

The book closes on Easter Sunday, 1928.

Dilsey begins the day by carrying wood, getting breakfast, and trying to maintain peace in the family.

There is a strange, dogged hopefulness about the woman as she ducks her gray head and heaves herself up and down the stairs at Mrs. Compson's whim.

But Dilsey gets her work done and goes off to church with her children and the feebleminded Ben.

The path is uphill and leads among dilapidated Negro cabins.

The weather-beaten church stands against a gray Easter morning.

Inside are decorations of crepe paper and above the pulpit an old red Christmas bell, the kind that folds up like an accordion.

The people sing, and then a preacher in a shabby alpaca coat gives a sermon on suffering and Easter, all about the agony of the cross, and about the golden horns shouting down the glory.

Dilsey weeps quietly, rises, and leaves the church.

Approaching the big Compson house, with its rotting portico, Dilsey's children want to know why she weeps.

She tells them never to mind and continues to weep what seem tears of comforted sorrow.

Back in the kitchen, about her usual tasks, from which there is no escape, she talks to herself about having seen the first and the last, the beginning and the end.

And Dilsey endures.

More than that, she lives joyfully, lovingly in the world, for she knows that her personal story is overshadowed by the story of God's salvation.

So Gabriel, lift your trumpet.

For though it often does not appear to be so, to eyes

of faith it is clear, especially when we wait on Patmos, or endure a world of rotting porticos, that "the Kingdoms of this world are become the Kingdom of our Lord and of his Christ, and he shall reign forever and ever." Amen.*

Hymn: "O God, Our Help in Ages Past"

---

4 The Evolution of Sermon Shape

"The Church of the Cryptic Cross" is one name that I have given to a contemporary building in another part of the world. That name comes from a cross in the chancel on which the "King of the Jews" placard is hanging by one nail, as though it were about to fall to the ground. I also call this "The Church of the Twin Pulpits" because it has two very large, matching ambos that seem to have been designed with dialogue preaching in mind. One preacher can stand in one, another in the other, and they can engage in a stationary form of dialogue preaching by speaking to each other with questions and answers, give and take, while the congregation listens in and, as Fred Craddock would put it, "overhears the gospel." Since the building is octagonal and not overly large, the congregation would be close enough to the speakers to become involved in the dialogue.

But it is the carvings on the wooden ambos that have intrigued me ever since I first saw them. Each of them contains a biblical scene in which the Good News is being proclaimed to a group of people. One scene depicts Peter preaching to the people in Jerusalem on the Day of Pentecost, as Luke reports that event (Acts 2:14ff):

> *But Peter, standing with the eleven, lifted up his voice and addressed them, "Men of Judea and all who dwell in Jerusalem, . . . give ear to my words . . . Men of Israel, hear these words: Jesus of Nazareth, a man attested to you by God with mighty works and wonders and signs which God did through him in your midst as you yourself know — this Jesus, delivered up according to the definite plan and foreknowledge of God, you crucified and killed . . . But God raised him up . . . Let all the house of Israel therefore know assuredly that God has made him both Lord and Christ, this Jesus whom you crucified."*

And Luke continues: "Now when they heard this they were cut to the heart, and said to Peter and the rest of the apostles, 'Brethren, what shall we do?' And Peter said to them, 'Repent, and be baptized everyone of you in the name of Jesus Christ for the forgiveness of your sins . . .' " And, according to Luke, about three thousand people repented and were baptized on that occasion.

On the other ambo, Paul is pictured preaching to the intellectuals at Athens (Acts 17:22ff):

> *"Men of Athens, I perceive that in every way you are very religious. For as I passed along, and observed the objects of your worship, I found also an altar with this inscription: 'To an unknown god.' What therefore you worship as unknown, this I proclaim to you.' "*

In the discourse that followed, Paul spoke of the God who created the world, asserting that people are "God's offspring" whom he now calls upon to repent "because he has fixed a day on which he will judge the world in righteousness by a man whom he has appointed, and of this he has given assurance to all men by raising him from the dead." Luke says that there was a mixed reaction to this claim: "Now when they heard of the resurrection of the dead, some mocked; but others said, 'We will hear you again about this . . . But some men joined him and believed.' "

The two graphic carvings show two different kinds of preachers speaking to two radically different audiences with diverse kinds of sermons, but the focus of each sermon is on the very heart of the gospel, the death and resurrection of Jesus Christ and what this event means for all people living in God's world. Although Peter and Paul told the Story within different types of story sermons, listeners could not misinterpret what they were talking about. They did not speak to entertain their hearers but to get their attention, reach their minds and hearts so that the Word and the Spirit could bestow the gift of faith upon them and change their lives. Primitive Christian preaching, as reported in Acts, was more like the telling of a story than anything else; it was narrative preaching. "The Church of the Twin Pulpits" reminds us of this and suggests a shape for our sermons today.

The Shape of Contemporary Preaching

Worship, in almost every denomination, not only has a new book, but it also has a new look. The new look and new book are quite similar in most of the liturgical churches; some elements of liturgical worship and preaching have even found their way into the practices of so-called non-liturgical churches. The increased use of the lectionary, especially the "ecumenical lectionary," is one proof of this. But while worship has many "common characteristics" among the denominations in America, preaching patterns show more diversity and, perhaps, disagreement on the function and shape of the sermon in today's pulpit ministry.

Elizabeth Achtemeier writes: "In general, preaching in the United States today takes one of four forms. There is first of all the approach that sees preaching as primarily a setting forth of the truth of biblical propositions; we could in fact label such preaching 'propositional preaching.' "[1] This sort of preaching, in her opinion, considers the Bible to be a set of propositions — "the Bible says," as Billy Graham and others use the phrase — to be proclaimed from the pulpit as "a set of truths" to be believed. The content of the sermons really has to do with the authority of the Scriptures. She does not deny that this type of preaching is effective and has led to the conversion of thousands of people to the faith, but she comments:

Nevertheless, leaving all other questions aside, the thoughtful preacher must ask why, if the Scriptures are really a set of propositions, they have been given to us largely in the form of stories? Has God's salvation of his world not been acted out precisely in the form of events?[2]

An understanding of the narrative nature of the Bible needs to become a mark of propositional preaching, as in black preaching that "even at its most propositional, . . . has preserved something of the narrative character of sacred history," if it is to remain a viable type of preaching.

Professor Achtemeier classifies the type of preaching "which is found in most mainline denominations . . . as 'thematic preaching.' " Thematic preaching, as she describes it, is really one type of modern expository preaching that some have called "sermonizing" and others have labelled "biblical preaching." It produces a sermon shaped around, or by, a theme that dominates thought and development usually in the form of the three-point sermon. She analyzes:

> *The presupposition of such "thematic preaching" in relation to the Bible is that there is a major idea or message which can be distilled out of the text, and the function of biblical criticism for such preaching, then has been to recover that major theme. That is, biblical criticism has been seen as the necessary tool for uncovering what the text really meant when it was written, and for years it has been the aim of many homiletics teachers to instill in their pupils the necessity of uncovering that actual meaning.*[3]

Achtemeier is convinced, apparently on the evidence of sermons she has read and heard, that "busy pastors have failed to do their exegetical homework" in the parish; it gets crowded out of the pastor's homiletical agenda by the myriad of other tasks that must be performed. And so, thematic preaching tends to be the proclamation of an *idea* discovered by the preacher in the text, and this is a major weakness with this kind of preaching. "The hermeneutical jump," Leander Keck's "priestly listening" (to the text), and a deficient theology of the Word, are among other problem areas in thematic preaching.

> *The message today of any biblical text is not simply its ancient meaning. Rather its message is the meaning which it has in relation to a congregation . . . for no event or Word of God in the Bible happens only in the past.*[4]

She is convinced that this is not what occurs in much thematic preaching.

It is her third type of preaching — "creative preaching" (which is the title of her book on story preaching — that Elizabeth Achtemeier believes "may hold the most promise for the future of preaching." By "the creative power of language and form, . . . the congregation can be enabled to 'live' the biblical story so that it becomes their story, creating the same salvific effects in their lives that that first story created in Israel and in the primitive church."[5] She contends that the "new hermeneutic" and the "new" literary criticism of scholars like C. H. Dodd, Amos Wilder, Robert Funk, Sally McFague, Robert Tannehill, and others, have — through their emphasis upon language and forms — taken the sermon beyond thematic preaching into various types of narrative preaching. She calls Frederick Buechner the "most widely known among such preachers," and included Fred Craddock, Edmund Steimle, Morris Niedenthal, Charles Rice, Richard Jensen, and James Sanders on her list of authors who are producing books about narrative preaching.

The fourth category which Achtemeier describes is "experimental preaching." It includes what she calls "a wide variety of substitutes for the traditional sermon," and she lists:

first-person sermons, dialogue and multilogue sermons, sermons formed from participation by the congregation, press conference sermons, dramatic monologues or multilogues, oral readings, mime, symbolic action, dance, verse sermons, imaginative parables or allegories, dialogues with newspapers or musical instruments, sermons formed from literature or hymns, use of various audiovisual aids in conjunction with the spoken word, folk-masses, religious musical dramas — the list is as endless as the human imagination.[6]

Her list offers evidence that the rubric in one experimental worship service — that "Exposition need not be confined to an address: other forms of proclamation — dialogue, drama, cantata, etc. — might also be employed" — was accepted by preachers. A text may, or may not, be read as the source of the sermon, and even if a text is the sermon's basis, too often the biblical story gets lost in the "experimental sermon." The people might be interested spectators or an involved audience in "something different" in Sunday worship, but do not participate — really — in the real Word-event that worship and biblical preaching make a present reality for the congregation. From the gospel's viewpoint, this may be a very unproductive way to preach, despite the fact that Elizabeth Achtemeier asserts, "There is room for experimental preaching in the church."

Any of the four types of preaching — propositional, thematic, creative or narrative, experimental — might be employed effectively in pastoral preaching, depending upon the kind of parish in which one preaches and how faithfully the preacher proclaims the living Word through the form that is employed for proclamation. But the "creative," or story sermon, when it is informed by biblical scholarship as well as communication theory and other contemporary concerns, is the most promising type of preaching for use within the liturgical worship of the church. The Story and the Song belong together in the liturgical life — gathered and separated — of the people of God.

The Evolution of the Story Sermon — the Beginning

In the past quarter of a century, the story sermon has had an evolutionary history of its own. Homileticians have always understood that the gospel is a story, and scholars like Paul Scherer, Richard Caemmerer, James S. Stewart, William Stidger, and a host of other writers and preachers have conceived of preaching as "telling the Story." But it was H. Grady Davis, in his *Design for Preaching*, who opened the way for the biblical story sermon to emerge as "the sermon shape for the future." Not only did Davis identify the functional forms — proclamation, teaching, and therapy — in his "1958 design," but he went on to change the categories of the biblical sermon from textual, thematic, expository — and their various combinations and variations — into what he named *organic forms*. He identified five such forms:

1. A subject discussed

2. A thesis supported

3. A question propounded

4. A message illumined

5. A story told

Davis explains the "a story told" type of sermon:

> *A sermon may take the form of a narrative of events, persons, actions and words. The distinguishing feature of this form is that the idea is embodied in the structure of verbal generalizations, whether assertions or questions.*
> *. . . But we preachers forget that the gospel is for*

the most part a simple narrative of persons, places, happenings, and conversation. Nine-tenths of our preaching is verbal exposition and argument, but not one-tenth of the gospel is exposition. Its ideas are mainly in the form of a story told.[7]

Davis was convinced that not more than 10% of the sermons that were being preached in the 1950s were narrative in nature, and he was also positive that, if his estimate was at all accurate, such story preaching received its impetus from the kinds of story sermons that the late Peter Marshall had delivered in the 1940s.

For some homileticians and preachers, Peter Marshall remains a controversial preacher three and a half decades after his death — a storyteller more than he was a teller of the Story. Study of his sermons reveals some of the obvious weaknesses of story preaching, as the variety of his sermon shapes suggests to anyone who has read Elizabeth Achtemeier's diagnosis of "creative" and "experimental" preaching. Marshall preached at least five different types of narrative sermons:

1. Biblical narratives — he retold, with little comment, the great stories of the Bible;

2. Life experience sermons — stories about people;

3. Autobiographical story sermons — as, for example, "The Tap on the Shoulder."

4. Sermons from stories, legends, literature — as "The Keeper of the Springs."

5. Some parabolic sermons.

That he was a great storyteller cannot be disputed.

Many of his sermons have to be called "post-textual;" some question if they should be called biblical sermons with one exception (No. 1 above). Not only the Bible as story, but other narrative forms influenced him. Grady Davis, however, pulled these various strands of narrative together into his "a story told" version of the biblical sermon, and the modern story sermon began to evolve.

The Deep Roots of the Gospel as Story

We may be certain that Davis knew of the emphasis upon the use of story in preaching by homileticians like William Stidger and preachers like Clarence Macartney; he was familiar with their books and their sermons. He undoubtedly had read Macartney's talk on "The Recall to Gospel Preaching." It begins:

Very early in my ministry I chanced to read in the British Weekly, *one of the most widely read religious journals, an article by the editor, Sir William Robertson Nicoll, in which he related his experiences in worshiping in churches in the south of England during a period of convalesence after a long illness. He spoke of the sober order and dignity of the services, and how the preachers were well-educated and sincere men who delivered thoughtful and carefully prepared sermons. But at the end of the article, he said: "Not one of them would have converted a titmouse." That sentence of indictment has often come back to me in the many years which have passed since I read that article — "Not one of them would have converted a titmouse." Across how many of our sermons, if the truth were told, would that indictment have to be written?*[8]

Macartney tried to get out from under that indictment in his own preaching ministry by preaching "for the conversion of the sinner to the will of God in Christ." He turned to narrative methodology in his preaching, becoming a master illustrator and storyteller. He discovered the power of biographical material in the Bible and preached sermons on biblical personalities in the belief that "the Bible is the supreme book on human personality." Clarence E. Macartney, as his books attest, effectively preached the gospel through story.

With William Stidger, who also recognized that the gospel is a story, a combination of the advent of radio and some advice from a famous preacher, Dr. S. Parkes Cadman, turned him toward the use of story in his preaching and his teaching of homiletics. The radio altered his style of preaching when he realized — long before Marshall McCluhan — that classical oratory would not work on the radio and that the more conversational style required by radio in speaking might be more effective in the pulpit. Dr. Cadman also advised him: "The wise preacher is the man who puts an abstract truth into a story, an illustration, or a parable; for then he may be certain that all of his hearers will get it."[9] The truth of that remark depends, of course, upon the impact of the story, its relevance to life, its qualities of imagination and involvement, and, of course, the skill of the preacher as a storyteller.

Stidger learned that lesson well, especially in developing the ability to turn ordinary incidents into stories, some of which became sermons. He wrote a series of books of sermon illustrations which were more like short stories than typical sermon illustrations; some were long enough to be called story sermons. One volume was titled *Sermon Nuggets in Stories*. In the introduction he wrote:

*As I travel through the church world, friends are
kind enough to ask me to autograph their copies
of my earlier books (of stories), and I launch this
new volume with several "autographs" in which
I have tried to set forth the purpose of my brief
stories . . .*

*When a mother or Sunday School teacher
tells me she likes to tell my stories to children or
young people,* I write: "Tell me a story!" is the
world-old cry of child, youth, and adult. Here in
these pages is the answer to that cry."[10]

Examination of sermons by the famous preachers of
that day reveals that most of them had discovered the
power of story — as sermon illustration, if nothing else
— in the preaching of the gospel. And many of them,
too, were master storytellers as well as biblical
expositors. This gave their sermons a narrative quality
not unlike one finds in at least one type of modern story
sermon, the Steimle model — "a story told" — in
Preaching the Story. But they were not story-preachers
in the sense that Peter Marshall produced and preached
narrative sermons, although their different — and more
limited — use of story prepared the way for the
evolution of the modern story sermon to begin.

Concentration Upon Thematic Preaching

Story preaching might have developed more rapidly
after World War II were it not for the impact that form
criticism made upon the study of the Scriptures in
numerous theological seminaries in the United States.
New interest in biblical exegesis was linked to preaching
— as it should be — with the result that thematic
preaching, as a development in expository preaching,
became an increasingly popular shape for sermons.
Preachers in liturgical churches as well as nonliturgical

churches felt the pressure to engage in thematic preaching. In 1949 Harry F. Baughman produced a volume, *Preaching from the Propers*, which became a handbook for thematic preaching in some of the liturgical churches. It was based on what might be called "comparative exegesis" of the liturgical propers — introit, collect, epistle, gradual, and the gospel — by which the central message of the day would emerge. It was a logical application of the new biblical methodology to the liturgical lessons in particular, but the theory could only be applied to those (few) sets of propers that had any thematic harmony. Baughman's thesis is a valid one for exegeting the "meaning of the day" in about thirty-five to forty percent of the lessons in the new lectionaries. It will not work during most of Epiphany and Pentecost when the second lessons are "out of sync" with the Old Testament and the Holy Gospel.

Printed sermons offer evidence that concern with the meaning of the text became such a dominant factor in thematic preaching that story was downgraded in favor of emphasis on the content of the sermon. One homiletician reached the conclusion that content really is all that matters in the sermon. "Get the content 'right' and you have a good sermon" is the way he phrased it. Less attention was given to the style and shape of the sermon, to the use of imagery in it, and to the way it was delivered in the pulpit. Clyde Reid's well-known — and scathing — analysis of the sorry plight of the Protestant pulpit in his *The Empty Pulpit* was a necessary indictment of preaching — and preachers — out of touch with the gospel as story. The 1960s was the decade that saw the renewal of preaching gain momentum again.

The Era of "Experimental Preaching"

Reuel Howe's *The Miracle of Dialogue* (1963) touched off a renewed interest in communication theory and a flurry of homiletical activity that sought to reshape the sermon so that the gospel might be communicated more effectively. *Partners in Preaching*, by Reuel Howe, was published the same day that Clyde Reid's *The Empty Pulpit* reached the bookstores.[11] When William D. Thompson and Gordon C. Bennett wrote *Dialogue Preaching: The Shared Sermon* (1969), experimental preaching was in high gear. John Killinger was among those who produced volumes of experimental sermons, some of which were his, but most of which were written by other preachers. He introduced one collection of experimental sermons this way:

> *The words "experimental preaching" suggest that it is a new kind of preaching. Actually it is and it isn't . . . There has always been experimentalism at work among authentic preachers. The central problem which all speakers face [is] of having something significant to say and discovering forms of discourse to shape the communication of that something.[12]*

The gospel is always a "given" in preaching, thus Killinger concentrated on the problem of sermon shape and effective communication of that gospel. Since I have already given Elizabeth Achtemeier's "endless list" of experimental sermon shapes and some of her warnings about built-in weaknesses, I will not attempt to reiterate or expand on what she has said. But it should be noted that "experimental preaching," almost in the face of "creative preaching" and story preaching, has spilled over into the 1980s, and some homileticians believe — with Achtemeier — that it should be encouraged.

Some of us took a more conservative approach to the renewal of the sermon. My own approach in *The Renewal of Liturgical Preaching* focused upon the content of the liturgical sermon from the perspective of church year and lectionary, but I included one chapter on "Preaching and the Shape of the Sermon" meant to be a call to alter the shape of the traditional (thematic) sermon through the use of story and parable. Many of the "guides," as I called them, are still useful and pertinent:

1. The preacher must . . . master the art of sermon illustration. Illustration is a requirement for effective preaching; it is not optional.

2. He will use the narrative form of proclamation.

3. He will usually employ the indicative mood.

4. He must recognize the importance of the metaphor in the Bible, and be able to use it himself. Other types of imagery may be almost as effective.

5. A brief sermon may in itself be a parable.[13]

The development of "the narrative form of proclamation" as a contemporary form for the sermon was left to others.

The Emergence of the Story Sermon

Preaching began to turn "the narrative corner" at the beginning of the 1970s and just as the new lectionaries were beginning to be employed in the churches. Thor Hall's *The Future Shape of Preaching* was an effort to integrate communication theory, theology, and exegetical methodology within the worship life of the congregation; he did not attempt to work out any new shapes — story or otherwise — for the sermon. That was left to Charles Rice in his *Interpretation and Imagination: The Preacher and Contemporary Literature*, which was an introduction into the narrative form of the sermon. Rice investigated the relationship of culture, literature, theology, and the content of the sermon, stating that "by way of suggesting the sermon's form, the preacher ought not to be embarrassed by story." And Rice also contends that "contemporary literature and Christian theology agree in the forms they suggest for preaching: story, a proper sequence between grace and ethics, indirection and understatement, the man as message." He argues that the narrative form "makes a large place for literature in the content of the sermon and gives story a prime place in the sermon's format." Arndt Halvorson's *Authentic Preaching*, which is described as "The Creative Encounter Between the Person of the Preacher, the Biblical Text, and Contemporary Life and Literature in Gospel Proclamation," unites sermon content and form — as Rice seeks to do — through story and literature.

But with the use of the new lectionaries in Protestant and Roman Catholic churches, story as a suitable shape for the contemporary sermon had to face increased pressure to concentrate on the content of the sermon. A veritable flood of exegetical helps for preachers using the three-year pericope system flowed from the publication houses, accompanied to a lesser degree by books of sermons on the new texts, but these, too, tended to be content centered. Little or no attention was given to the shape of the sermon even in excellent exegetical homiletical commentaries such as the *Proclamation* series of Fortress Press. Exegetically informed content is fundamental to the proclamation of the gospels, especially in the new lectionaries, but the content may be lost in the communication process if the shape of the sermon — and how it is preached — should be neglected.

Fortunately, preaching received an assist in finding forms for proclaiming the gospel to congregations through the insights and efforts of homileticians like Fred Craddock, Milton Crumm, Clement Welsh, Frederick Buechner, Foster McCurley,[14] Clyde Fant, and others. These writers and their works helped to correct the homiletical excesses brought out in some attempts at experimental preaching by stressing the importance of the biblical content and the organic form of the sermon. Narrative — and the story sermon — began to emerge as a legitimate sermonic shape for gospel preaching.

The year 1980 saw the publication of three volumes about the story-shape of the sermon, all of considerable importance for preaching. Elizabeth Achtemeier's *Creative Preaching: Finding the Words* deals with language and creativity which are faithful to the biblical witness in preaching texts. She really pulls together the diverse strands of homiletical thought from the previous decade, and evaluates them from the perspective of biblical scholar, homiletician, and preacher. She insists on leaving the homiletical door open for experimentation in sermon language and form as long as the preacher is under the mandate to do careful exegesis in a biblically enlightened manner. She concludes:

Creative preaching finally happens only when God in Christ lays hold of our lives and works his transforming new creation in heart and mind and action. Then words catch fire, and love is born, and the Christian community becomes reality;

and God presses forward toward the goal
of his kingdom on earth. I only know that God
does so act, if we are faithful to him.[15]

Richard Jensen, a systematician, produced the second volume, *Telling the Story*[16] reveals his homiletical intention in the subtitle, *Variety and Imagination in Preaching*. From an analysis of some of the weaknesses of contemporary preaching that is similar to that of Clyde Reid, Jensen suggests three types of sermons for "telling the Story" — didactic, proclamatory, and story sermons. But it is the story sermon that Jensen concentrates upon and really is interested in motivating pastors to imitate or develop on their own. Jensen combines Grady Davis' first two functional forms — proclamation and teaching — with his fifth organic form — a story told — but his treatment of the story sermon has more similarity to some of Charles Rice's story sermons than it does to the intentions of Davis when he writes about "a story told." The story must begin with the Bible: "Always begin with a text. Story preaching must be anchored firmly in a given text(s) of Scripture." Jensen opens the "evolutionary door" a bit farther with his *Telling the Story*.

Proclaiming the Story, the third book on story preaching to appear in 1980, takes up Grady Davis' "a story told" organic form for the sermon and gives it contemporary expression throught Edmund A. Steimle, Morris J. Niedenthal, Charles L. Rice, and five other preachers, all of whom were former students of Steimle while he taught at Union Theological Seminary, New York. Chapter 10, "The Fabric of the Sermon," delineates the story sermon — "a narrative in all its parts" — as a biblical sermon that *faithfully tells the story* — not the theme or even the message — of a

Scripture passage. It could be called a modern expository sermon, and specifically a modern method of doing a running commentary. As William J. Carl declared in response to Don M. Wardlaw's "Eventful Sermon Shapes," a multiverse text preached in story fashion "means returning to a kind of expository preaching."[17]

Has the sermon gone "full circle" in its evolutionary process so as to return — better informed biblically and theologically, perhaps? Has the shape of the sermon actually become more in touch with the gospel as story? Or does "a story told" represent a genuine evolutionary advancement in the shape of the sermon, and will it assist preachers to proclaim the gospel more effectively today? Does *Preaching the Story,* as the culmination of the evolution of the story sermon since Grady Davis in 1958, have a weakness built into it by limiting the "a story told" kind of sermon to a single narrative shape? And will the "a story told" story sermon inspire the people, who have come together to worship God and respond to his gift of grace in Jesus Christ, to sing their song of praise and thanksgiving in the liturgy? It is obvious that we must look at the story sermon — and its varieties — in more depth and detail.

An Example of "a Story Told" Biblical Sermon

When Edmund A. Steimle delivered two of the chapters (7 and 10, of *Preaching the Story* as lectures at the January, 1978, convocation of Luther Northwestern Seminary, St. Paul, Minnesota, he also preached a sermon to demonstrate his conception of the "a story told" type of biblical narrative. It was called "The Stranger," and it is printed in a collection of sermons entitled *God the Stranger*. The thirteen sermons in this book were also preached on the National Radio Pulpit (NBC) from April 2 to June 25, 1978. Except for the introduction and one illustration pertaining strictly to the clergy, "The Stranger" was preached to a radio audience in exactly the same form and language employed when it was delivered to some five hundred pastors and professors in St. Paul. It is worth studying over against *Preaching the Story* and, particularly, Chapter 10, "The Fabric of the Sermon." If the chapters, (seven and ten especially) are read after reading the sermon, the reader has approximately the same opportunity to react to Steimle's description of the "a story told" type of story sermon — as those who heard the lectures and the sermon in January of 1978.

"The Stranger" was the second sermon preached in the radio series (for the Second Sunday of Easter) and was developed from the familiar Luke 24:13-35 text. The Easter Sunday sermon — on Mark 16:1-8 — was called "Easter — Festival of Mystery," and introduced the theme of the thirteen sermon series, "Reflections about Resurrection." Steimle's goal was to help people "see more of the mystery and intrigue of Easter — and perhaps end up wanting to sing more carols." He contrasted the one day celebration of Easter, as most people seem to observe it, with the extended celebration of Christmas in which "the whole world is turned on its ear . . . and for weeks at a time," declaring, "It's strange, really. For if there were no Easter, there'd be no Christmas . . . no New Testament, no church, no Christianity." And then he asks the question which he tries to resolve in the sermon: "So why does Easter cut so little ice in the world today, compared with Christmas? Steimle asserts that the mystery can be faced only "out of the corner of the eye." Easter is embarrassing, for God works through death and the Cross; Easter brings judgment before it gives joy, and the word that precedes the gladness of Easter is, "Be not afraid." The resurrection makes us face death and suffering and sin, and "only then comes the joy (of Easter)." "The

Stranger'' picks up the mystery and examines it from Luke's perspective.

"The Stranger"
Edmund A. Steimle

That very day two of them were going to a village named Emmaus, about seven miles from Jerusalem, and talking with each other about all these things that had happened. While they were talking and discussing together, Jesus himself drew near and went with them. But their eyes were kept from recognizing him. And he said to them, "What is this conversation which you are holding with each other as you walk?" And they stood still, looking sad. Then one of them, named Cleopas, answered him, "Are you the only visitor to Jerusalem who does not know the things that have happened in these days?" And he said to them, "What things?" And they said to him, "Concerning Jesus of Nazareth, who was a prophet mighty in deed and word before God and all the people, and how our chief priests and rulers delivered him up to be condemned to death, and crucified him. But we had hoped that he was the one to redeem Israel. Yes, and besides all this, it is now the third day since this happened. Moreover, some women of our company amazed us. They were at the tomb early in the morning and did not find his body; and they came back saying that they had even seen a vision of angels, who said that he was alive. Some of those who were with us went to the tomb, and found it just as the women had said; but him they did not see." And he said to them, "O foolish men, and slow of heart to believe all that the prophets have spoken! Was it not necessary that the Christ should suffer these things and enter into his glory?" And beginning with Moses and all the prophets, he interpreted to them in all the scriptures the things concerning himself.

So they drew near to the village to which they were going. He appeared to be going further, but they constrained him, saying, "Stay with us, for it is toward evening and the day is now far spent." So he went in to stay with them. When he was at table with them, he took the bread and blessed, and broke it, and gave it to them. And their eyes were opened and they recognized him; and he vanished out of their sight. Then they said to each other, "Did not our hearts burn within us while he talked to us on the road, while he opened to us the scriptures?" And they rose that same hour and returned to Jerusalem; and they found the eleven gathered together and those who were with them, who said, "The Lord has risen indeed, and has appeared to Simon!" Then they told what happened on the road, and how he was known to them in the breaking of the bread. (Luke 24:13-35)

The story of the walk to Emmaus is one of the loveliest stories in the New Testament, certainly the most intriguing of the appearance stories following the Resurrection. But it has positively sinister implications for you and me some two thousand years later. If the risen Christ walking and talking with two of his disciples is unrecognizable, how are you and I ever to recognize God's presence with us today? If the risen Christ is a stranger to his own disciples, how much more of a stranger will God seem to us twenty centuries later?

That part of the story, that he was not recognized, is baffling. Presumably they have been in daily contact with him for the better part of three years. And now they do not even recognize him. What goes on here? Was he wearing a disguise? But what of his voice? His familiar clothing? His mannerisms, the way he walked? All those familiar characteristics of a close friend that lead us to recognition even after years of separation — but they had been separated for only three days. "But their eyes were kept from recognizing him." Why was this so?

Well, for one thing, we have to remember that it was the *crucified* Jesus who was raised from the dead and appeared to the disciples. And it was the crucified Jesus whom they were unprepared to recognize as the Christ, even before the death. Remember, "they all forsook him and fled." And if they were unprepared to recognize him for what he was in death, they were equally unprepared to recognize the crucified Christ in the appearances after the Resurrection. After all, if he was the Christ, God would not let him die, would he? And die in disgrace at the hands of the religious establishment in Jerusalem? It was all too much.

And after it was all over and they were making their lonely way to Emmaus, even if the tales of the women having seen him alive were true, he wouldn't appear as a stranger along the road with them, would he? Where was the blinding Resurrection light? The angels? The hallelujah chorus? It was all far too ordinary, too undramatic, calmly interpreting Scripture to them as if nothing had happened, like some hotshot Christian whipping out his pocket New Testament to tell us what the good old Book really has to say. So "their eyes were kept from recognizing him." Their eyes were kept because of their preconceived notions of how God would and would not act. They were blinded by their expectations of how God would and would not act.

But this was nothing new, really. This had been so before the events of the past three days. Jesus was different. He met no one's expectations. As Hans Kung writes:

> He did not belong to the establishment nor to the revolutionary party, but neither did he want to opt out of ordinary life, to be an ascetic monk. Obviously he did not adopt the role which a saint or a seeker after holiness, or even a prophet, is frequently expected to play. For this he was too normal in his clothing, his eating habits, his general behavior . . . [So he became a] skandalon, a small stone over which one might stumble . . . He was attacked on all sides. He had not played any of the expected roles: for those who supported law and order he turned out to be a provocateur, dangerous to the system. He disappointed the activist revolutionaries by his nonviolent love of peace . . . he offended the passive, world-forsaking ascetics by his uninhibited worldliness. And for the devout who adapted themselves to the world he was too uncompromising. For the silent majority he was too noisy and for the noisy minority he was too quiet, too gentle for the strict and too strict for the gentle. He was an obvious outsider.
> He was different — a stranger.

And if all this was true then, why should it be any different now? If Christ is really the clue to who and what God is and how God acts, God will not fit into *our* notions of how God should and should not act either. Most of us tend to domesticate God, that is, make God fit into our notions of how God should act. So God becomes the patron saint of a democratic, capitalist system. God blesses America and hates the communists even more than we do. God becomes a gargantuan, blown-up version of *me* in my better moments. God should be comfortable and folksy; close, not far; forgiving, not judging; giving us comfort and peace of mind rather than asking us to deny ourselves and follow him.

A couple of years ago I was giving a series of sermons during a week at a summer assembly. At the end of the week an elderly gentleman came up and after some complimentary remarks about my preaching went on to say that he didn't agree at all with one of the sermons, in which I had attempted to point out that God in his nearness can be known only in contrast with God in his distance, based on Isaiah's startling vision of God in the temple filled with smoke and the song of the seraphim: "Holy, holy, holy is the Lord of hosts." He said to me, "God is not far . . . I've got him in my heart." Very cozy. There is a sense, of course, in which God *can* be known in our hearts, but the God of the Bible, the God revealed in the living Christ, also stands over against us in our "hearts." We do not take him captive in our hearts. Indeed *he* may take *us* captive in our hearts, and then perhaps we can know the peace of God which passes all understanding. But it is precisely beyond our understanding, because God, if Christ is the clue to his nature, is different. He is surprising, like appearing as a stranger along the dusty road to Emmaus.

Now there is a strange sort of comfort in all this. Perhaps when we are baffled by the way God apparently works in our world, he may be closer to us than we realize — as the disciples discovered when they arrived at Emmaus: "Did not our hearts burn within us while he talked to us along the road?" So even in our experience of the absence of God, there may be the experience of his presence — as Tillich points out — "in the empty space that cries out to be filled by him." So when prayer goes unanswered, or we are overwhelmed with tragedy — with cancer or a crippling stroke or the family falling apart — or there is senseless terrorism and grinding poverty and blatant racism, the fact that our experience or lack of experience of God points to a mystery, the mystery of *no* experience of God in the way in which we expect, precisely *there* may be the possibility of meeting the stranger along the road.

But before the story ended, the stranger did become recognizable in the breaking of bread. They had invited him in to stay with them. And "when he was at table with them, he took the bread and blessed and broke it and gave it to them. And their eyes were opened and they recognized him."

For the early church there is little question that this pointed to the experience of the living Christ in the Sacrament, the Eucharist. And that may also be true for us. As the community of believers gathers about the table set with bread and wine, and we hear the ancient words, "Take, eat; this is my body . . . take, drink; this is the blood of the New Testament," and are reminded both of the death and at the same time of the hope of a great banquet in the future, our eyes may then be opened too, so that we recognize the stranger for what he really is.

But such recognition may not be limited solely to the cultic act of the Sacrament. No doubt it was the familiar words or gestures that did it. The familiar words of the blessing may come to us today in reassurance and hope on the lips of a familiar friend or a member of the family or even a preacher. Or the family words of the blessing may come to us in the expression of care and concern by someone familiar to us, and we are comforted and encouraged and given hope. Reminded of days and hours when God was familiar rather than strange, we are encouraged and given hope that Christ is indeed alive, and that God, for all his strangeness, is faithful to his promises to be with us always, even to the end of the age.

Or contrariwise, the stranger may be recognizable when you and I respond in love and concern and thoughtfulness to the needs of another. As John says in the Fourth Gospel, "He that wills to *do* shall know." I can remember in my last parish that when I was down in the dumps, discouraged, uncertain of the reality of God, I would go to the hospital and visit with patients from my parish, offering what I could of reassurance and comfort and hope in God's presence and care, and then the God who may have been a stranger to me earlier became recognizable in the breaking of bread.

But it may be that he becomes recognizable on the lips of unlikely people. It was many years ago, shortly after the end of World War II, and I was in the shop of a friendly neighborhood tailor whose name was Mr. Birnbaum. And he stopped me as I was leaving and said in his thick accent, "Mr. Steimle, I have a problem. As you know, I am a Jew and my wife, she is a Christian. Her brother was a violent Nazi when we were in Germany. He hated me and did nothing to help us. He was happy to get rid of us when we came over here. But now he is in a prison camp and he has written us asking us to send him some food. My wife, she says No, we send him nothing. But I say Yes, we should send him something. What do you think, Mr. Steimle?" I don't know how you would have felt, but I felt humble and ashamed. Ashamed of his Christian wife possibly, but even more ashamed of myself for being unprepared to find the stranger God recognizable on the lips of a pleasant Jewish neighborhood tailor.

And then the story ends abruptly: "And he vanished out of their sight." Which is to say, you can't nail God down to a dining room table and the breaking of bread any more than you can nail God down to a cross with real nails, for that matter. They wanted him to stay. They wanted to rehash this marvelous experience. But God would have no part in deadly-boring postmortems, as at a bridge table; "he vanished out of their sight."

"The stranger comes suddenly out of nowhere (as another puts it) like the first clear light of the sun after a thunderstorm, or maybe like the thunder itself, and maybe we recognize him and maybe we don't." But maybe we can reach the point where we can bless God not merely for his recognizable presence, but precisely because he is different, unpredictable, breaking away from our stultifying expectations, precisely because he does come as the stranger into our lives to give assurance and pardon and hope.*

---

*"The Stranger" by Edmund Steimle, from *God the Stranger,* Copyright © 1979 by Fortress Press. Used by permission of Fortress Press.

5 The Importance of "A Story Told"

Churches tell stories of God and his people. They are repositories of the history of God's relationship to those who, for centuries in some instances, have met to hear the Word, been renewed by Christ through the Holy Spirit, and have sung their songs of praise in response to God's goodness and grace. They tell of God's faithfulness and forgiveness — testify to his continual patience with humanity — in the face of price and perfidy. The stories are told in different ways: some have to be extracted from the records and histories of the congregations; other stories are passed on and perpetuated orally; still others are contained in, and live on in, the symbolism and the works of art that decorate them. The great cathedrals of Europe told their stories on their facades and interiors with sculpture and bas-relief, paintings and stained glass. A local, three-decade-old church building has made an exceptional effort at story telling in its windows. They attempt to tell the whole story — God's and ours.

This church building — Gloria Dei Lutheran Church, St. Paul, Minnesota — seems a bit out of place in this mid-section of America because it is done in colonial style. It looms large, elevated on a man-made mound of dirt covered with grass; it is, for a parish church, imposing and interesting. Many features commend it as an excellent example of this type of architecture, but the pastel-hued windows, particularly, speak to preachers. Most church windows depict biblical scenes and concentrate on telling the story of God's attitude and actions toward the human race, highlighting the gospel with interpretations of the life of Christ worked into the glass. Gloria Dei's windows are different from most in that they recreate and retell the human story from the creation to the middle of the twentieth century in the perspective of the biblical story. They chronicle the beginnings and development of the Christian church in the world by picturing the Apostles, the Church Fathers, saints and martyrs, servants of the church — musicians, scholars, humanitarians, inventors — so that their stories might be remembered in conjunction with the biblical Story and, especially, the gospel. The uniqueness of these windows is that they are like "a story told," as Edmund Steimle expands this concept of the narrative sermon, "in all of its parts."

For example, the window closest to the chancel pictures the drama of the Crucifixion. Christ on the cross dominates the upper half of the window. Below his left arm is a smaller scene showing him in the Garden of Gethsemane and praying, "If it is possible, let this cup pass me by. Nevertheless, let it be as you, not I, would have it." (Matthew 26:39) Beneath Christ's right arm is a cameo-scene of Christ being condemned to death by Pilate; no words are necessary to remind the viewer of that part of the story. But Jesus' word about discipleship is divided in two and put alongside each of these passion-death events: "If any man would come after me, let him take up his cross daily and follow me." The lower half of the window illustrates how people have followed Christ as obedient servants. Unnamed martyrs are there, but there is also a preacher in a pulpit, a teacher in a classroom, a nurse tending a patient in a hospital, a mother offering cookies to her two children, a draftsman at a drawing board, a scientist in his laboratory; some are in modern garb, others are in colonial or medieval clothing. All of the windows in the nave have this "mix" of biblical and secular story; one of the windows even depicts the Bomb exploding over Hiroshima as a warning to those who see it and as a call to repentance. If it were possible to add a new window today, it would tell the story of what has been happening in the world in the last thirty years — astronauts and men on the Moon, medical miracles, computers and jumbo jets, famine and disease and the energy crisis, migrant workers and displaced persons — and the Bomb — over against the Parousia affirming that Christ is the hope of the world. Another window will always be needed for the continuing human story until Christ returns and ushers in the fulness of the Kingdom and, with that, gives the Story a new twist as he comes to reign in glory. The windows in this church building might be termed a paradigm for one type of story sermon — "a story told" — through the combination of biblical and secular stories.

The Story Sermon: Power and Limitations

In their quest to improve the communication of the gospel in Sunday worship, preachers and homileticians have rediscovered the power of narrative sermons to engage people emotionally and imaginatively in the preaching event. The story sermon avoids proclamation that is intentionally intellectual in character by involving the whole person in the story that is told. When the narrative sermon combines the stories of the Word and the world into a unified message, homilies powerful enough to interest and actually change people may result.

In his *Pastoral Counseling and Preaching,* Donald Capps contends that story, especially the parable, is an effective tool to employ as a counseling method. He identifies three methods of biblical counseling — the Psalmic, the Proverbic, and the Parabolic — and argues that the latter has the greatest potential for effective pastoral counseling. Something "happens" in a parable or a story which alters the relationship of people participating in the event, because the meaning of the event "is communicated *through the story itself, especially its details.*"[1] He points out that the meaning is woven into the story or parable, not added on, and because it is open-ended, the counselee reaches his own conclusion as insight is gained into the story and the person's own situation. Capps calls this a "transformative" method which restructures perceptions and the ways that people look at life. Much of what he suggests by drawing upon the work of James E. Dittes[2] and applying it to counseling is applicable to preaching and the story sermon. Although Capps prescribes theological themes for preaching, he does not suggest parabolic or story methodology for the proclamation of the gospel, as H. Grady Davis recommended a quarter of a century ago. A host of homileticians and preachers agree with Davis today.

Davis discovered, in his study of sermons, that not all types of story sermons are equally viable for the preaching of the gospel, not even Peter Marshall's. His best story sermons, according to Davis, were biblical narratives, concluding that Marshall has "some success" with them. "Pure-narrative" sermons may leave the gospel remote from the people; the Word may be indistinct or inaudible — not articulated by the preacher's story or heard distinctly by the listeners. Nor are sermons shaped as wholly biblical narratives always effective; they may make no connections with the lives of people dwelling in a world radically different from that in which Jesus lived. Davis believed that such biblical story sermons might best be reserved for the great festivals of the church year, while preachers might employ story in other ways in their weekly preaching regimen.

Grady Davis, while convinced that preachers ought to engage in more narrative preaching, was aware of the problems inherent in story preaching. First, he understood how story works in sermons; many preachers don't. Story conveys meaning indirectly through characters, conversation, confrontation, and interaction. Story "speaks by suggestion rather than in direct and explicit statement, " eliminating the "direct and explicit assertion," that is (in his opinion) a stock item in the preacher's homiletical methodology: "A little too much preaching quickly destroys the inherent force of the narrative."[3] This means that the preacher has to trust the story and learn how to master a rather sophisticated sermonic form — "a story told" — while keeping it simple and clear. The modern biblical narrative calls for creative, as well as exegetical and theological, skills to be highly developed in the preacher to assure that the gospel will be proclaimed.

Second, story sermons demand "more active listening" by the hearers than do other types of sermons. The sermon has to be so constructed that "the hearer . . . identifies himself with the characters in the story, lives through the incidents with them, understands their motives, and renders his own verdict on their opinions, character, and actions . . ." If the audience only hears "a story," they will probably miss the message that the preacher intends them to hear. "Yet," Davis suggests, "the teller of the story must trust the people to comprehend the meaning of the story they are hearing and, hopefully, living."[5] Most preachers seem unwilling to do that, even in an occasional — and simple — retelling of an episode in the gospel on special festivals or rare occasions.

For these and other reasons, Grady Davis did not recommend all types of story sermons "for everyday use" nor for every type of text. With Richard Jensen, he reserves them for the occasional sermon, and tends to assign them to preachers with whom story is "a natural form." Edmond Steimle believes, too, that story sermons other than the "a story told" type of sermon are done best by "those who have the gift" — and that such story sermons "can be effective."[6] Steimle suggests that the alert and informed parish preacher needs a type of story sermon that may be utilized in a preaching ministry Sunday after Sunday. That's where Steimle's development of Davis' "a story told" fits into the homiletical picture as the best type of story sermon for telling the Story to people today.

"A Story Told" — Revisited

Preaching the Story was written by eight persons but it deals with one type of narrative sermon — the biblical story sermon that H. Grady Davis described as "a story told." This is not surprising since the assignment given to Edmund Steimle and the others was to update *Design for Preaching,* which had been the most widely used text in homiletics almost since it was printed in 1958. With the current emphasis on story in biblical and systematic theology, in addition to some seminal works on story sermons, a book on narrative preaching was highly desirable. Davis' term for the biblical sermon — "a story told" — set the theme for the new book and set it aside from other attempts to produce a volume on narrative preaching. A holistic approach to contemporary preaching was needed, the team of homileticians and pastors decided, and further development of the "a story told" sermon shape could accomplish that.

As *Proclaiming the Story* was conceived, a holistic view of preaching would involve four different conceptions of preaching: 1) preacher-centered preaching; 2) person-centered (the hearers' needs) preaching; 3) context-centered preaching; and 4) content-centered preaching. Considered separately, each has its strengths and weaknesses. Morris Niedenthal and Charles Rice contend:

> *The content-centered view tends toward incomprehensible jargon . . . and a mechanization of the grace of God; the preacher-centered view toward egotism and subjectivism; the institutional view toward the promotion of something other than the gospel; and the need-centered view toward superficiality.*[7]

They also acknowledge the strength of each view of preaching:

> *The preacher-centered view acknowledges the power of example, the importance of personal investment in interpretation, and requires honesty in the preacher. The need-centered view keeps the message "relevant." The community-oriented view takes seriously the family of God in ways that it is possible for other approaches to avoid, and the content-centered approach, in its very insistence on the truth, honors implicitly the God who is the truth.*[8]

The model of preaching that would pull these diverse elements together, it was decided, was that of the *storyteller* with an audience gathered around him attentively listening to a story that is interesting and important because it involves them. That story is the biblical story and, in particular, the gospel of Jesus the Christ. Perhaps the biblical sermon should be called "*The* Story told." (Steimle always capitalizes The Story in the book.)

But Steimle also calls the Bible "The Story of Good and Evil" (Chapter 7) because it is the story that "begins with the conflict between good and evil, between God's good will and humanity's refusal to accept and live by that will."[9] It is the story of humankind's rebellion against God — the Fall, sin, and separation from God and one another — and how God deals with that rebellion. The stories that are part of the narrative are meant to "evoke faith in God" as a return to him, and reaching the climax of the story in the New Testament story about Jesus Christ with its exhortation, "Repent and believe in the Lord Jesus Christ." It is at once the story of God's faithfulness and grace, of the depth of his love for his creatures and, especially, for humankind — his children. And while the story contains judgment, too, it also gives the resolution of the conflict in the obedience "unto death" and the resurrection of Jesus Christ.

The task in preaching today is to "rehearse this story week after week until it becomes a part of us." That makes story preaching liturgical preaching; "a story told" — as a model for the biblical story sermon — has always been aware of the signals from the church year that call for the telling of The Story of Jesus Christ *in kerygmatic perspective* — his death and resurrection — to evoke faith, spell out God's judgment, his mercy, and the grounds he has given the world to have hope in Christ. *Preaching the Story* doesn't say so explicitly, but the liturgy and the church year virtually demand narrative preaching from the pastors charged with the proclamation of the gospel. Domenico Grasso's comment that "Man must listen continually to what God tells him through the mouth of his heralds . . .

listening to preaching is therefore the best form of worship that man can render to God," needs amplification. If Karl Barth could sum up all that he had learned in the study of the Bible and theology with "Jesus loves me, this I know," then the preacher who has been informed kergymatically by that Bible, in combination with the church year, should sing, "I love to tell the Story . . . of Jesus and his love." The response of the faithful — "I love to hear the Story" — is what makes listening to a sermon "the best form of worship that man can render to God." The Story spells out the good news mysteriously revealed in the life, death, and resurrection of Jesus Christ.

When Edmund Steimle contends that the "fabric" of the sermon — its form and content — both need to be biblical, he is urging narrative sermon shape upon the preachers of the Word. He says, "The fabric or texture of the sermon, as well as its content, will be determined by its biblical roots," which is story. And he rightly reminds us that preaching The Story is not merely a recital of the events — God's mighty acts — in the past, but the announcement that God is real and present right now, "making his claim and offering his grace." Rather than the form-follows-function methodology that Grady Davis prescribed in his *organic forms* (proclamation, teaching, and therapy) and functional forms (a subject discussed, a thesis supported, a question propounded, a message illumined, *and* a story told), the argument that Steimle develops from Amos Wilder, Dan Via, and other New Testament scholars, is that the biblical sermon is shaped by the Story-form of the Bible — "form follows form." When story is more than "merely a recital" of the gospel, and The Story is contemporary, the "storyteller" image combines the form-follows-function (Davis) theory with the content-follows-content and the form-follows-form theory of Steimle. The sermon ought to be "like a story told in all of its parts'' to qualify as a biblical sermon, and, more importantly, to proclaim the good news — tell The Story with power and fidelity.

The fabric of the biblical story sermon, according to Edmund Steimle, has four characteristics:

1. First, the fabric of the biblical witness is completely and thoroughly secular . . . The story is told as if God were at work in the world, which of course and indeed he [is] . . . This means in explicit terms that the sermon will be studded with allusions to the facts and fancies and news events which make the newspapers . . . [10]

2. If the sermon is to be biblical, the fabric will not only be secular but also dialogical . . . It is crucial that the sermon identify the blindness of the preacher with the blindness of the congregation. Otherwise a dialogue may be taking place between the preacher and the congregation rather than between the preacher-congregation and the Word of God. [11]

3. [A] third characteristic of biblical rhetoric will be that it takes the form of a story told, as a whole and in its parts.

   . . . the dramatic form of a biblical address will affect the structure of the sermon. Each sermon should have something of the dramatic form of a play or short story . . . [and] at its deepest level it will draw us into the development of a plot or story. [12]

4. Finally, the fabric of the sermon will be as lean and spare as the fabric of the Bible . . . [This] will force us to cut and trim the words we use, the juicy adjectives, the fancy alliterations, the

quoting of hymns and of sentimental religious poetry, and the abstractions — especially the abstractions.[13]

This last might be the most difficult part of story preaching, simply because so much of the biblical drama is communicated to us in abstract language (creation, incarnation, redemption, atonement, resurrection, forgiveness — and "even sin and grace"). The proper use of the narrative in the sermon will overcome the use of abstractions and also make the sermon "lean and spare."

The "a story told" approach to the biblical sermon that was suggested by Grady Davis a quarter of a century ago has been developed by Edmund Steimle in a manner that is consistent with biblical scholarship, theological insight, and homiletical evolution — and it accommodates liturgical worship. When The Story is told in this manner, the people will sing the Song of thanksgiving, praise, and faith.

A Way to Shape the Biblical Story Sermon

More and more preachers are asking today, "How do I construct a biblical story sermon?" "What is different about it from the kinds of sermons with which I am familiar?" "How can I be certain that I will be preaching the gospel and not simply telling a story?" Story preaching, preachers seem to realize, is not an easy way out of the drudgery of sermon preparation or a short-cut to attaining excellence in preaching. That's why these and other questions are being put to homileticians and, especially, to those authors who have written about narrative preaching. The questions need to be addressed, I suggest the following procedure.

First, *unravel the plot of the biblical story.* "Plot" is the word for the narrative structure of a story which is

made up of "smaller narrative structures or episodes."
Dan Via reminds us that narrative fiction locates people
and what they do in the world of imagination through
the plot of the story, and that in Western literature the
plot is either comic or tragic. He informs us that plot is
the controlling factor in the parables and that the
preacher should never forget that the Bible is in the
form of a story, "a narration in time — and this fact
suggests that the biblical view of life itself is in the
nature of a dramatic plot."[14]

The plot of a biblical story embraces the characters,
the action, dialogue, encounter between protagonist and
antagonist, thought, and resolution of the conflict.
Story always has a beginning and an ending, but the
encounter takes place in the middle section of the plot.
Biblical story has both comic and tragic elements in it,
but it must be classified as comic because God has
provided the solution to the conflict between good and
evil in the person of Jesus Christ. The Story surrounds
the little stories of the Bible with a framework that is
hopeful and positive, and the little stories — the
pericopes, if you will — concentrate on part of the plot
and amplify it within that (kerygmatic) framework. The
Story itself is in the low mimetic mode in which realism
is to be found and gives, on the descriptive level, "as
clear and honest an impression of external reality as is
possible."

The study of the plot finds the preacher asking
questions of the particular pericope that is to be the
basis of the story sermon: "What is this incident all
about?" and "What's the encounter, the conflict in it?"
— and, says Via, "How will it turn out?" By asking
such questions of the text and its plot, the preacher
uncovers the story line which becomes the outline, or
plan, of the story sermon. The plot offers and controls
the shape that the biblical sermon will assume through
the preparatory and constructive efforts of the

preacher. As the pastor allows it to speak to him or her, the plot marches him/her through the text according to the action, the encounter, the conflict, and the resolution of that conflict in the liturgical lesson. This biblical story sermon resemble the classic sermonic form of the running commentary. An example follows this section.

Second, *identify the theme of the story.* Plot isn't the sole factor that the preacher must consider in the modern narrative sermon. If it were, a purely narrative biblical sermon of the Peter Marshall type would result. The "a story told" kind of story sermon, like "all narrative literature, contains both plot and theme or thought in some relationship." Via calls plot and theme the "two sides of the same formal principal with plot being theme in movement and theme being plot at a standstill."[15] Theme requires preachers to ask, "What is the point?" or "What does this (story) mean?" Such questions bring the flow of the story to a temporary halt and allow the theme to expand under the force of proper exegesis of the text *and* in the light of the contemporary conditions in congregations and the world. *Exploration and exposition of the biblical theme transform the purely biblical narrative into the more useful "a story told" type of biblical story sermon* in week-to-week proclamation of the gospel.

The theme or thought of the sermon, as distilled from the pericope, is necessary if the sermon is to edify, as well as interest, the people who hear it; it serves to stir up the imagination so as to involve them in the preaching event. Development of the theme gives relevance to the message by suggesting concrete applications to life today, thereby eliminating any abstractions that might make The Story seem remote to the current-day congregation. This is where illustration becomes very important to the story sermon; *it allows expansion of the thought in the story mode rather than through explanation* or *exposition.* The sermon remains a story sermon through the use of "our stories," simultaneously permitting an appeal to the intellect as well as to the emotions of the hearers. Theme offers the opportunity to develop theological depth in the story sermon when it is considered in this manner.

Third, *develop the structure, or outline, of the story sermon from the combination of plot and theme.* The sermon is shaped, basically, by the plot of the text while the theme informs the preacher where to stop the story and expand its theme for the benefit of the congregation. The theme plays down detailed retelling of the biblical story but it emphasizes the importance of allowing it to speak to the people with meaning and impact. Unlike the running commentary type of sermon, the biblical story sermon — "a story told" — does not give "equal time" to each verse or every part of the biblical text; plot and theme suggest to the preacher what should be eliminated as well as what should be emphasized or highlighted. But a good outline takes its beginning, its development in the middle of the story sermon, and the conclusion, from the combination of plot and theme — always, of course, in the context of the larger Story, the gospel of Jesus Christ. It will have a good movement, follow the storyline of the text, and will be marked by simplicity and clarity, unity and cohesiveness. The structure of the sermon will be that of a short story rather than an essay, a lecture, or a lesson in the form of a didactic sermon. Its thrust is on the telling of the story, not on the "points" or the meaning of the text. It is essential that the outline-structure be properly developed if the sermon is to be like "a story told." (Notice the simplicity of the outline-structure in Steimle's "The Stranger.")

Fourth, *interweave the stories of people, preacher, and contemporary life with The Story as it is contained*

in the sermon text. It is important to the story sermon
that at least some of the illustrations are in the form of
"little stories." Elizabeth Achtemeier insists that
illustrations are of critical importance to the sermon,
but she also says that they should be "rather short" by
which she means a couple of sentences in length. This
can create a problem for the hearers simply because they
have little opportunity to participate in them by
reflecting upon how they affect their faith and lives. In
standard types of sermons, illustrations serve to *clarify*
the message of the sermon and the meaning of the text,
but in story sermons their function primarily has to do
with involving and stimulating the hearers so that they
find the meaning for themselves as they think and live
out the stories in the context of pericope and the gospel
— The Story. They turn the Story toward the people.
Such illustrations and stories must be of high quality,
marked by *realism, substance, drama, action, dialogue,
and meaning.*

Interweaving the stories of people and preacher with
The Story requires a high degree of sensitivity,
perception, and skill on the part of the preacher, the
storyteller. It means that preachers will have to devote
time to mastering the art of sermon illustration as an
essential element in the homiletical process of "a story
told" sermons. A later chapter will deal with this
important ingredient in the narrative sermon process.

Fifth, *write the sermon in manuscript form* after all
of the above steps have been completed in the planning-
production process of the story sermon. This should
assure that the preacher will be writing in an oral form;
story is an oral mode of communication. Preachers will
improve their storytelling skills and their story sermons
if they consider this an inherent step in the total process.
Eliminating the writing of the sermon, as more than a
few persons suggest in the quest for an oral style, does
not necessarily guarantee that the preacher will achieve

such a goal. In addition, by writing out the entire sermon, the preacher will control the length of the sermon on Sunday morning, have an easily accessible record of sermons that have been preached, and a visual manuscript to study in the learning-delivery phase of the homiletical procedure.

Sixth, *learn the sermon so that it can be told from the pulpit essentially as it has been planned and written.* Remember that stories are meant to be told, not simply read to people; story sermons are included in this dictum. Almost any sermon is more effective when the use of the manuscript is reserved for the learning portion of the process. Story sermons, especially, deserve (if not demand) to be told orally to the congregation. A later chapter will deal with learning and speaking the story sermon as an integral part of any holistic approach to preaching.

The type of story sermon that is produced by this kind, or similar types, of process is what I — along with John Killenger[16] — call a "meat-and-potatoes" style of preaching that can be employed in the weekly round of pastoral preaching. Other kinds of story sermons may be conceived, planned, and produced *occasionally* and for special situations, but biblical narratives in the shape of "a story told" are the most useful type of sermon for preachers and their people. This is one preacher's method of developing them.

Anatomy of the "A Story Told" Sermon

Part of my assignment for one of the 1982 Lutheran Conferences for Worship and Music was to prepare and preach a sermon within a "demonstration" funeral service. The theme for this and the other conferences was "The Caring and Celebrating Congregation"; the context was that of the new book of occasional services for the *LBW* which was introduced in the fall of 1982.

Specifically, the service was to be eucharistic, the lections were assigned from "The Burial of the Dead" in the *Lutheran Book of Worship*, and the text for the sermon was John 11:21-27, the familiar story of Jesus' raising of Lazarus from the dead. In addition to theological lectures and workshops on the occasional services and pastoral preaching, sermons on the three preceding evenings had been delivered by the conference chaplain, the conference dean (a wedding sermon), and the theologian (on healing and wholeness). The preachers of the marriage sermon, the sermon for a healing service, and the funeral sermon were asked to duplicate their sermons and distribute them to the pastors present before they were actually preached. Discussion of the sermons was planned for the following day.

When I read and studied the assigned text from the Gospel of St. John, I immediately realized that it lends itself to the "a story told" type of biblical story sermon. First of all, it has an interesting and intriguing plot. Lazarus was very ill; his sisters sent for Jesus but instead of going immediately to Bethany, he dismissed the illness as an "illness not unto death" but through which "the Son of Man will be glorified." He waited a couple days before he said to the disciples, "Let us go to Judea." When they questioned him, he replied that Lazarus had fallen asleep — and then told them plainly that Lazarus was dead; he was going to raise him. Martha met Jesus outside of Bethany with the tone of rebuke in her voice: "Lord, if you had been here, my brother would not have died." Christ told her, "Your brother will rise again." When Mary repeated Martha's words in Bethany, Christ asked to be taken to the tomb and, over their objections — "he has been dead four days" — asked them to roll away the stone and commanded, "Lazarus, come forth." He did — after Jesus, who had wept openly before the grave, lifted up his heart to God in prayer. The plot then gets more complicated when the chief priests and Pharisees got together, discussed the danger Jesus posed for them and the faith, and decided that Jesus had to be eliminated. The assigned text deals only with the confrontation of Jesus by Martha, but, I decided that the context had to be kept in mind, if not actually included in the sermon.

The theme of the passage is relevant and important for people to grasp today. When Martha answers Jesus' reply with, "I know he will rise in the resurrection on the last day," Jesus says, "I am the resurrection and the life. If anyone believes in me, even though he dies he will live, and whoever lives and believes in me will never die. Do you believe this?" Her answer comes as a confession of faith — that Jesus is the Promised One and has come into the world at last. The raising of Lazarus would be (and was) an act of resuscitation, not resurrection; Christ would be the first to experience God's power in a resurrection. And while many of us face death in our loved ones — or ourselves — with Martha's "Lord, if you . . . ," faith in Christ assures us that the new life we have experienced with him in baptism will be ours in the Day of Resurrection. The development of the theme in these seven verses of John's Gospel clearly stops the action and suggests how the story-theme might be developed in the sermon.

The strategy of the sermon came from the encounter and the ensuing dialogue between Martha and Jesus, as well as Jesus' brief speech about the resurrection. The outline had to include the encounter, the conflict, and something of the resolution of the conflict through Jesus' words and actions. The action needed to be stopped and the theme expanded at, "Lord, if you had been here" and "I am the resurrection and the life" — and a clear distinction needed to be made between resuscitation and resurrection for the hearers and, if it were a real funeral, the mourners. The message should bolster their faith and encourage their "I believe . . . " The outline is simple and, I trust, clear and uncomplicated as "a story told."

The stories of people and pastor used in the sermon are compact, with one exception — the story about the student who suffered a heart attack. A couple of them have been adapted for this sermon;[17] they have been in other published sermons of recent vintage and would not be known to many of the audience attending and participating in the worship workshop. The episode from the film *Reds* is in a collection of sermons (*The Man, The Message, and The Mission*) that had not been published when this sermon was preached; it reached printed form two months later. The combination of The Story and the little contemporary stories makes this a sermon that the preacher should find rather easy to preach without notes — to *tell* the story-sermon, if you will. These elements ground the "Lazarus story" in contemporary life, helping to make the story-message memorable.

The sermon, as it was preached at the "funeral service" in the worship conference, could have been called "A Death that Was Not to Be," but the title I used was simply "Grave for Sale."

"Grave for Sale"
John 11:21-27

Martha said to Jesus, "Lord, if you had been here, my brother would not have died. And even now I know that whatever you ask from God, God will give you." Jesus said to her, "Your brother will rise again." Martha said to him, "I know that he will rise again in the resurrection at the last day." Jesus said to her, "I am the resur- rection and the life; he who believes in me, though I die, yet shall he live, and whoever lives and believes in me shall never die. Do you believe this?" She said to him, "Yes, Lord; I believe that you are the Christ, the Son of God, he who is coming into the world."

Some time ago, a strange classified ad appeared in a newspaper in one of our cities. It began: "Tombstone for sale," and continued, "Didn't die; don't need it." A reporter investigated and interviewed Art Kranz, the man who had placed the advertisement in the paper. Kranz told him that the tombstone had been sitting in his living room for several months, but it was not his; it belonged to his sister, who had been gravely ill with terminal cancer. An orderly person, she made arrangements for her funeral, including the purchase of a tombstone, a cemetery plot, and chose a funeral director. But she didn't die. She recovered, asked her brother, who had a pickup truck, to move the tombstone and sell it. First, he stored it in his living room, then moved it to the front porch and ran the ad, "Tombstone for sale," in the hope of finding a buyer for it.

When Jesus approached Bethany that day long ago, there was no "grave for sale" or "tombstone for sale" sign in sight. Instead, he was met by Martha, who confronted him with, "Lord, if you had been here, my brother would not have died." Lazarus was dead, and Martha knew that Jesus had been aware of the illness that threatened him with death: Hadn't she and Mary sent a message to Jesus out of desperation, informing him of Lazarus' plight? But he didn't respond. Martha must have been shocked when, later on, she heard the rest of the story: How Jesus had declared to his disciples, "This illness is not unto death; it is for the glory of God, so that the Son of God may be glorified by means of it"; and how Jesus stayed at the Jordan two more days before he told them that Lazarus was dead and *only then* said, "Let us to to him"; and how Thomas, typically for him, answered, "Let us go and die with him." Lazarus was dead; Jesus had let him die!

Martha and her sister, Mary, expected their brother's death and probably thought they were prepared for it, but they were still hoping for a miracle through Jesus. All through the last half of the movie, *Reds,* the audience was being prepared for Jack Reed's death. His wife, Louise, made a long and arduous — and forbidden — journey to Petrograd, Russia, where they enjoyed a brief reunion before he was hospitalized. After he slipped into a comatose state, he called out deliriously. And then, miraculously, he regained consciousness and talked lucidly to his wife. He asked for a drink of water just before he fell asleep again. She touched his forehead before she left the room to refill the water container. Louise had to walk some distance through the crowded corridors; sick and dying peasants seemed to be lying in every available space. On her way back to Jack's room, the camera seemed to focus on a woman she had passed before; she had set up her private chapel — with icon and cross — and was conducting her prayers to Almighty God, perhaps for all the sick persons in that hospital. But Jack was beyond help, and when Louise reached his room, she saw a doctor folding his arms across his chest. Louise, toward the end of the movie, unclasped them, held one hand in hers as she sobbed out her grief and pain, unable to articulate with Martha and Mary, as we do so often, "Lord, if you had been there . . ."

But all Martha got from Jesus when they met near Bethany was a promise after she had said to him, "Lord, if you had been here, my brother would not have died." Jesus told her, "Your brother shall rise again." And, when Mary met them and added her, "Lord, if you had been here . . . ," to Martha's plaintive words, Jesus asked where his tomb was, wept, and went into action. Mary hadn't heard him say, "I am the resurrection and the life," or "he who believes in me, though he die, yet shall he live," or "whoever lives and believes in me shall never die" — but that didn't seem to matter to Jesus. At the tomb, he commanded them to roll away the stone and called out, "Lazarus, come forth!" And he did. He was alive again. Grave for sale! Tombstone for sale! And isn't that how we would like Christ to eliminate death for us?

Not so. After all, Lazarus was resuscitated, not resurrected, and all we know of him after this is that he surely died again. Resuscitation was not enough in his case, nor is it in ours. Our need is for faith in Christ and his resurrection — that, through God's love and grace, we will be lifted up to new life in the age to come through the one who said, "I am the resurrection and the life; he who believes in me, though he die, shall live again, and whoever believes in me shall never die."

Death will claim us as it did Lazarus. Resuscitation is not enough, as a twenty-four-year-old student of theology discovered. Toward the end of a touch football game a couple years ago, he suddenly experienced a severe pain in his chest. Gradually, it went away. After a short rest, he and his wife and another couple went out to dinner. They were waiting to be seated when the pain returned; it was so severe that he had to find a chair and sit down. He had the presence of mind to realize that his condition was serious and said, "Better get me to a hospital." Fortuitously, they were near a famous "heart hospital," and they got him there and into the emergency room very quickly. But on the examining table his heart stopped beating. He was dead — briefly — but they resuscitated him. He said later: "The last things I remember were the feeling that I was going to die; I knew it. The pain was intense, unbearable, but I wondered what was going to happen to my wife. And then, suddenly, I knew that I had nothing to fear . . . and the last thing I heard the nurse say was, 'We're losing him.' " He had burns on his chest when he awakened, but he was alive. "The pain was gone and everything looked bright and new again."

He has also said, "Most of my old questions about death and resurrection are gone; now I have a new set of questions. Baptism means more to me than it ever has before; it has taken on a new meaning for me and my life." He is able to say, "I believe in Jesus Christ" and connect his faith with life and death, because Jesus' "I am the resurrection and the life" means more than it ever did. He was resuscitated, but he firmly believes that he will be resurrected through the mercy and grace of God in Jesus Christ. What more can we say and believe when we dare to, or are forced to, look death in the eye?

If you and I had heard only the latter part of this story in which Jesus raised Lazarus, we'd have no real hope at all. We'd be in the situation that William Saroyan found himself in five days before he died several years ago. He called the Associated Press and said to a reporter: "Everybody has got to die, but I have always believed that an exception would be made in my case. Now what?" You see, we don't stand in front of Lazarus' grave saying, "Lord, if you had been here my brother — or I — would not have died." We enter Jesus' tomb — through baptism — and rise with him, nurtured by his spirit so that we can grow and be firm in the faith that the God who loves us and gave his Son for our forgiveness and deliverance, will never let us go — will never let us die. We live in the Christ who said, "I am the resurrection and the life." Jesus did not eliminate death; he defeated it through the resurrection — for all of us.

A few years ago, a Jesuit professor of theology in Rome said to me, "If you want to see what Italian Christians believe, go out and visit our cemeteries." My wife and I did just that — went to the Campo Verano, the only cemetery being used in Rome today. In the old part of the cemetery, we discovered that every grave was above ground. Most had flowers (it was All Saints' Day), some had photographs, and each had an "eternal light" burning as though to say, "I believe . . . in the resurrection of the dead." When we went into the new section of the cemetery, we discovered high-rise mausoleums which looked — on inspection — like tidied-up catacombs with photos instead of bones — and flowers and eternal lights declaring, "I believe in the resurrection — through Jesus Christ." And then we found our way into the fourth century church of St. Lawrence — San Lorenzo — and learned that the martyr who gave up his life for Christ still lies under the altar — and that catacombs extend like fingers from under that church-tomb (tombstone for the entire population?) to all parts of the cemetery, and I understood the Jesuit professor's words. The entire cemetery seems to be poised in the faith that Christ will return, open the graves, and will raise up those who believe in him to new life in his eternal kingdom. The place seems to say: "Graves for sale. Tombstones for sale. Soon." And isn't that we can say, through faith? "Tombstone — grave — for sale. *Did* die — in baptism with Christ. Now live in him through grace and faith. Don't need them now!" Amen.

6 Sermon Illustration in the Story Sermon

A few years ago I used to drive past an unusual church building at least a couple times a week. It could be seen from one of the interstate highways leading to an airport in the city suburbs. Some people said it looked like a modified Chinese pagoda. Others simply said that it looked strange. An article in the newspaper reported that it was an attempt to give architectural expression — in a church building — to Durer's familiar "Praying Hands" painting. After reading that story and seeing the sign that was placed near the high-way — House of Prayer Lutheran Church — not only could I see the prayer motif in the building, but it became a kind of sermon in stone for me, one that triggered thoughts and memories whenever I passed by it after that.

One of those memories was of my paternal grand-father who lived in our home the last seventeen years of his life, passing ninety-one before he died. He was a patient, genuinely pious man who read his Bible daily — and marked every page again and again as diligently as a biblical scholar. He learned to pray as regularly and devoutly as any cloistered monk or nun. A Methodist all of his life, he knew nothing about liturgy or liturgical prayer, but he knew the Kyrie intuitively. Time and again I heard him pray, "Lord, have mercy upon us." Years later when I studied the liturgy in the seminary, I realized that I had already learned it from my grandfather. His devotional reading and studying of the Bible and his pattern of private prayer belong in a course on spirituality. The Word of God and prayer sustained him in troubled times, carrying him through deep personal anguish to the end of his days. To the very end, he lived by the love and grace of God, enduring in hope.

The sight of House of Prayer Church brought back other memories, too. Among them is an incident that occurred when I was a pastor in Harrisburg, Pennsylvania. The men in our parish annually staged a banquet to honor the football players in two local high schools. The nave of the church was above a parish hall half in and half out of the ground. Since tables and chairs filled the parish hall, the men and boys had to gather in the church nave to await the call to dinner. With their interest in dinner and the awards to be given, they stood around in little groups or sat in the pews, talking and laughing, anticipating a good time.

I happened to be standing near the door when one of our members came in with his son and young daughter; she was the only girl in attendance (her mother was in the hospital). She had never been in the church building before because she and her mother were Roman Catholic while her father and brother were Lutheran. She looked around the nave and was surprised by what she saw. "Your church is like ours — and it's beautiful," she said to her father. "And you have an altar just like we do; it's beautiful, too," the six-year-old girl added. But then she looked around the nave again, taking in the light-hearted bantering in the groups of men and boys awaiting the call to dinner. She turned back to her father again — and I felt she was addressing me, too

— and asked, "But why aren't they praying?" At her tender age, she knew one thing about how church buildings are to be used as places of worship: "My house shall be called a house of prayer for all people." For her, indeed, the church was a house of prayer.

On the rare occasions when I pass House of Prayer Church — and it is more difficult to see now because other structures have been built between the church and the freeway — and I am reminded of those incidents and others, I find Tennyson's poem working its way into my thinking:

> *More things are wrought by prayer*
> *Than this world dreams of . . .*

And the last two lines remind me:

> *For so the whole round earth is very way*
> *Bound by gold chains about the feet of God.*

And on those occasions when I have preached on Matthew 21:13 in the context in which our Lord quoted Isaiah 56:7, stories like these find their way into my sermons to enable people to perceive what the Word is about and help them to participate in The Story that is being told.

Rethinking the Art of Sermon Illustration

Sermon illustration has always been considered an important, if controversial, element of an effective sermon. The great preachers have nearly all demonstrated proficiency in the art of sermon illustration. But it has also been controversial among homileticians and theologians; both have warned against the "excesses" of sermon illustration. A young theologian once took aim at the pastor of a very large Lutheran church in the

United States by criticizing his preaching. He called him "just a storyteller." To the theologian, the pastor's use of illustration — especially anecdotes — in his sermon was degrading to the pastoral office and denigrating to The Story, the gospel. The thousands of people who attended worship in that church heard more than "just a storyteller"; they would tell you that they were hearing this preacher tell The Story. Few would say that he used stories to excess in his sermons.

Illustration is especially important in the biblical, "a story told," type of narrative sermons. The stories of people and the preachers are an integral part of the narrative sermon, according to Edmund Steimle. They help to create the fabric, the *textus,* of the sermon through a weaving process — *texare,* "to weave — in the construction of it. When Andrew Blackwood used to talk about the *warp* and the *woof* in the sermon, he was thinking primarily of the same thing Steimle addresses:

> *To describe preaching as storytelling does not mean that the sermon becomes a clothesline hung with anecdotes. Nor does it mean, necessarily, the creation of a modern parable-story . . . What it does mean is that the preacher is involved in the sensitive interweaving of three stories: 1) the preacher's own, 2) the listener's story, and 3) the Bible's story, usually in the form of a pericope or passage which may be a sub-story of the great biblical story itself.* [1]

The kind of biblical narrative sermon that Steimle presses preachers to adopt for their preaching ministries, especially in liturgical churches, involves the use of illustrations, or stories, as Steimle simply calls them.

Elizabeth Achtemeier picks up on this in her *Creative Preaching:*

The question to ask of an illustration, . . . is, Does this enable the congregation to identify with the biblical story? Good illustrations may grab a congregation at the beginning of a sermon by showing them that the text is about their lives, and then more illustrations may sustain that interest throughout the entire length of the delivery by making every point crystal clear and by forming pictures of its concrete meaning in the people's mind. [2]

She believes that "good illustrations, by personalizing the biblical message, may drive it home to some reluctant heart." And they just might "catch the mood of the congregational response to the Word, may give voice to the faith the sermon has aroused and verbalize the people's 'yes, yes. Oh, yes!' " Illustrations are as essential to The Song as they are to the telling of The Story.

The genius of story when it is used as sermon illustration is that it functions the way that all good stories do when they are told well; it invites people to participate in the story. Story involves people in a little slice of real life, with people who can laugh and cry, succeed and fail, live and die as we all do. Stories in the sermon allow the listeners to identify with the biblical story and to respond to it in their own way; they are a way of reliving The Story and the little stories, the pericopes, in our own personal lives. Good illustration might provide the sermon with the four classical effects of imagery — interest, beauty, truth (or clarity), and completeness[3] — or it may function in the sermon in any one or all of the seventeen ways that serve the sermon event,[4] but its greatest contribution to story preaching is that, as it involves people in The Story, they can live their own stories and discover how the gospel relates to them.

This is why a sermon illustration has to be extended

in length beyond the simple metaphor or simile, or even the picture, to the story, as C. H. Dodd observed happens in the Bible in Jesus' parables and stories. The problem with pictures — or rather brief illustrations — is that a picture is action that is stopped and captured in one scene, a still life. It depends upon the preacher's powers of description. But a story is actual life. It contains movement and drama, action and encounter, and its characters think and speak and act out their emotions and their thoughts. A story may simply be told; it does its own work when it is well told, and when it is told in sufficient detail. Questions and answers, confrontation and resolution of conflict, moments of meaning and revelation, words and actions that mirror how people live in the world, and characters who are as real as we are, catch us up in the story so that we might comprehend and live The Story. If illustrations are too brief, resembling cartoons more than real stories, they seldom permit people to participate in them with any depth of experience and meaning.

On the other hand, if sermon illustrations are extended too far and become overly long, they may easily lose their power to involve people. Longer illustrations have to be carefully crafted by the preacher. They must have sufficient detail and drama and dialogue to allow people to get involved in them, but should be short enough to retain their force and focus. The one-page short story is a good model with which the preacher may experiment, attempting to reduce it even farther without destroying its impact and appeal to the hearers. The secret of mastering the art of reducing any short story to a length that is suitable for a sermon is in making it your own story by allowing it to come to life in the imagination. Once the preacher has "lived" the story this way, it is relatively easy to shape it appropriately for the sermon. It should have more impact through literary and homiletical tailoring.

And story allows reflection to replace the kinds of explanation with which sermons tend to be overloaded — and which make so many sermons "dull and deadly." Commentary upon the Bible gives way to perception about life as children of God. Story as sermon illustration transforms the pulpit lecture into a genuine Word-event for the worshipers because it stirs up both mind and heart so that preaching and worship together become a real and dynamic experience in their lives.

Reworking the Theory of Illustration

The interweaving process employed in the biblical narrative requires reworking of the older theory of sermon illustration in books like Sangster's *The Craft of Sermon Illustrations* or Ian Macphersons's *The Art of Illustrating Sermons.* Macpherson's theory could be classified as *mechanistic* from the manner in which he sets out the *mechanics* of sermon illustration that the preacher needs to master to become proficient in the art. His chapters discuss the *functions* of illustration in the sermon, *finding* illustrations and classifying them, *filing* them systematically, *fabrication* of the paragraph-illustration, *fitting* them into the sermon, and *facilitating* their effective presentation in the pulpit. His is a helpful theory, a useful system, and a standard approach to the business of learning how to illustrate sermons.

This standard system of sermon illustration is a functional system. It has these marks:

1. The *paragraph* is the unit of illustration;

2. The *function* of the illustration is to clarify and emphasize an idea or a truth;

3. Illustration is *limited* and *closed;* its one point is pre-determined by the idea or truth it supports;

4. It is literally *biblical* — "the best illustrations for a sermon are found in the Bible";

5. Illustration is *optional;* other literary devices may be employed in place of it;

6. Illustration, generally, is *added on* to the idea or truth it is to illustrate.[5]

A newer theory of illustration emerges when illustration is considered in the framework of the narrative sermon. Some of the characteristics are:

1. *The entire sermon,* rather than the paragraph, may be the unit of imagery-illustration — a kind of stretched metaphor;

2. Illustration becomes a *vehicle* of communication that conveys an experience instead of a functional device;

3. It is *open-ended,* allowing the hearer to participate freely in it and reach meaning for himself;

4. It is *genuinely biblical* because, like the Bible, it is secular, grounded in contemporary life;

5. It is *indispensable,* not optional, to avoid casting the sermon in the past tense as well as to avoid the "dull and deadly" trap in preaching;

6. Illustration is *built into* the fabric of the sermon that is being prepared.

The older theory complements thematic and topical sermons; the newer theory is necessary if one intends to preach narrative sermons and, in particular, "a story told" biblical narrative. And it is entirely possible to transfer the name "standard" to the biblical story sermon instead of limiting its use to the non-narrative types of sermons. Then it would be the "standard theory for biblical narratives or story preaching."

Rediscovering Autobiographical Story

The majority of preachers, I suspect, welcome all the help they can obtain in locating good illustrations and discovering effective ways to work them into their sermons. One of the main reasons that preachers read books of sermons is that most of them provide illustrations — or "helps" — that the harassed pastor can easily adapt and use in his sermons. All kinds of illustrative materials seem to be acceptable but good stories are preferred. The preacher never seems to have too large a supply of stories and illustrations; time, pastors tell me, just isn't available for the reading they know they should do. Commentaries are the shortcut in exegetical and content matters, and sermon collections provide ready-made sermon illustrations. Some of them don't even need to be rewritten; they are simply transferred from one page to another. No one is embarrassed to use other preachers' stories.

Many preachers do avoid one type of illustration, the personal story; autobiographical illustrations seem to be the kind of sermon illustration that preachers shy away from in their sermons. "I don't want my people to think I am preaching about myself when I should be preaching the gospel," one pastor remarked in a seminar on story preaching. Confided another, "I was trained to think in terms of 'you and I' or 'we' when addressing the people directly in the sermon, and I suppose that has conditioned me not to speak about myself or my experiences as a human being.''

A sermon is always the gospel according to one particular preacher because the pastor always speaks as a believer, a witness to the grace of God as the gospel has come to him, and not only as one set aside to proclaim the Word. There is something wrong if a preacher does not ask occasionally, while stepping into the pulpit, "What in the world am I doing up here preaching the gospel to these people?" Nevertheless, the preacher has a story to tell — and it must be told.

Steimle insists that the preacher's story must be told — by the preacher and in the sermon:

> *The preacher's own story appears, of course, in every sermon explicitly or implicitly . . . It is important, at least on occasion, for the preacher to speak explicitly of his or her own story, doubts, anxieties, perplexities, his or her own agonizing with the implications of the faith, if for no other reason than to reassure the congregation that the preacher is indeed one of them and not above them . . . In evaluating sermons in preaching workshops across the country, I am often struck by their flat, impersonal tone as if the preachers who wrote them were dealing with material that had never touched or engaged them personally.* [7]

And so he advises that "the personal story, used judiciously, can serve to break down the barrier between the preacher and the listeners." This means that preachers must use personal stories with sensitivity and also with skill.

In an unpublished paper, "First Person Narrative Preaching," Richard Thulin suggests that autobiographical preaching is more complex than it may appear to be. The reason is that there are four types of narratives — personal stories — that may be used in story preaching. The first, *illustration,* is "a brief first person narrative which is used to clarify or confirm a general statement." This is simply standard sermon illustration theory, taking into account the possibility of preachers inserting stories from their own experience to illustrate their messages.

Reminiscence is his second category: It is "a narrative of a thing remembered, a person or incident, but it is usually concerned with private relationships rather than public events." He says, "The incidents which it recounts are really 'things of memory,' from a more or less distant past, while those recounted by illustration may be quite current."[8] Thulin observes that reminiscences are more detailed than illustration, have more emotional content, and "seem more significant to the teller." Reminiscences may still serve the truth of the message, but they also have meaning in and by themselves. There is truth in the incident or event.

Thulin calls the third category *confession,* which has nothing to do with baring one's soul and confessing one's sins to the congregation, nor does it speak of one's personal convictions. It has to do with personal spiritual experience and struggle, "or of the workings of God's providence in vocation or personal life . . . It focuses on the self . . . (and) reveals the narrator in intense engagement with God." Reminiscence remains on the human-to-human plane of existence. He differentiates further:

> *The confession moves beyond the reminiscence in another point also. The intention of reminiscence is frequently to make an appeal . . . The confession seems to intend as much as anything the setting forth of an example.*[9]

For Thulin, the ultimate function of the confession would seem to be to encourage others by offering "a pattern for belief, action, and attitude." The preacher "encourages the (hearer) not by some conclusion he has drawn from a remembered event, but by the remembered event itself."[10]

Self-portrayal, according to Richard Thulin, "is the most comprehensive form of first person narrative. It includes key aspects of each of the other types, particularly those of the reminiscence and the confession, and unites their varying emphases while often moving beyond them."[11] He delineates between them:

> *Self-portrayal focuses on the self not only as thinking (reminiscence) and feeling (confession) but also as willing . . . It also focuses on the self in the totality of its relationships, its relationship with God-cosmos (confession) and its relationship with other selves, with the natural world, and with human culture (reminiscence).*[12]

Self-portrayal has to do with self-analysis, discovery of identity, self-acceptance, and "the achievement of human integrity." It comes from an experience that *results in personal change and a kind of new beginning.* " It differes from the illustration, the reminiscence, and the confession in that "the narrator does not simply remember a past event or person, but remembers himself or herself within the event and reflects on himself or herself as remembering." By simply telling the story this way, the listener is given the opportunity to respond for himself or herself and relive the event in the imagination, or remember a similar experience in his or her own life. This may take the hearer beyond the story of the preacher so as to discover something about self, relationship to God and to others not comprehended before — and change may take place as edification and growth in the faith.

Edmund A. Steimle's "Mr. Birnbaum" story is the

example of self-portrayal that Thulin uses in his paper, pointing out that the incident occurred some thirty years before it was included in the sermon. The tailor's penetrating question, "What do you think, Mr. Steimle?" focuses our attention on his internal reaction, not so much to the tailor's question (which, incidentally, Steimle never answers in the sermon) as to the situation out of which the question came."[13] He remarks:

> *Steimle portrays himself as both feeling and thinking (and perhaps in a later paragraph a self that wills when he suggests that he can come to bless God because he does come as the stranger into our lives). He makes the connections for us between his inner and outer worlds. Steimle also shows himself in relationship to both other people and to God, even though he does not tell us the nature of God's presence (we may assume both as judgment and grace), nor the effect this incident had on his future relationship with the tailor and others.*[14]

Professor Thulin may be quite correct when he concludes that this might be a way for Steimle to put the incident "to rest by putting it into a definitive framework." The listeners are given the opportunity to live it as he tells it, to dredge up a similar incident in their own lives, or join Steimle in his reaction — surprise and some shame — which "can be both education and catharsis."

That type of personal story avoids the impersonal quality of much sermon illustration, permitting the preacher to give a kind of personal testimony in which God — not the preacher — is really the subject of the story and the sermon. The preacher gave no advice, answer, or comfort to the tailor; he only revealed himself to be a human being like all the people listening to

him or reading it in *God the Stranger.* If, as Richard
Thulin suggests, first person narrative self-portrayal is a
"theoretical form" for contemporary preaching,
Steimle demonstrates how to shape autobiographical
incidents into stories that people will listen to eagerly
and respond to wholeheartedly. And we are reminded
that first person narrative stories are as necessary as the
people's stories if pastor and people are to be in
dialogue with The Story.

On Becoming a Storyteller

Some of us seem to be "born storytellers," but most
of us have to learn this art that is of such importance for
preaching. "Tell me a story!" is the universal cry of
little children as bedtime approaches. More than an
attempt to stall the process of going to sleep for the
night, and more than a desire to be entertained, the request comes from deep inside these little persons
because they need to learn about parents, other people,
life, death, and God. Story teaches our children about
those things that really matter to us human beings; it is
also a way that they participate in the past, the present,
and anticipate the future with hope. Some of us learn to
love stories as children, and when this happens, potential storytellers are created.

Listening to stories tends to diminish as we begin to
grow up. Our teenagers *listen* to rock and roll; they
listen to — and tell — stories about what is going on, as
do most adults. People *watch* and listen today, as far as
stories are concerned. Television shows the story instead
of merely telling it; it seems to make the telling of stories
obsolete. Even theological students sometimes say of
the wonderful stories in the Bible, "I've heard them
all," implying that it is time to go on to something else.
They don't seem to realize that all we have is A Story. I
suspect that the problem is not simply overfamiliarity

with Bible stories and the gospel, but that many of them have forgotten how to listen to a story.

Storytelling begins with listening — with learning to love the stories that all sorts of people try to tell us. For those who preach, storytelling begins and is rooted in The Story and, especially, the gospel of our Lord. That Story helps us to love stories that we hear, but more than anything else, when The Story takes over in our lives, we eagerly become storytellers — "I love to tell the Story . . . of Jesus and his love."

Since the preacher has to interweave our stories and The Story in narrative preaching, it is necessary to become a *reader* of stories. Even if we heard the Bible stories when we were young, we need to reread those stories later on — and often. Nikos Kazantzakis tells of his thoughts when he was invited by a cardinal of the church to go to Rome to study for the priesthood:

> *I remained silent. The face of Christ had fasci-nated me indescribably ever since my childhood. I had followed him on the icons as he was born, reached his twelfth year, stood in a rowboat and raised his hand to make the sea grow calm; then as he was scourged and crucified, and as he called out upon the cross, "My God, my God, why hast thou forsaken me?" After that, as one fine morning he rose from the tomb and as-cended to heaven, clasping the white pennon in his hand. Seeing him, I too was scourged, I too was crucified and resurrected.* And when I read the Bible, the ancient tales came to life . . . (emphasis mine)[15]

Thus, a storyteller was born.

But storytellers have to read more than the Bible, especially if they are preachers. They need to read the sermons of master preachers, the stories of the great storytellers in literature, and the tales told by columnists and feature writers in the daily newspapers and periodicals. They need to read all sorts of stories because they represent life as it is lived and people as they really are.

Storytellers have one thing in common — developed perception; they see what is going on around them in the world and they attempt to understand it and then tell it as story to others. They look for the ordinary and the important happenings in life — and for connections between them. They gather together the events that matter to — or disturb — them and shape these things into stories. They see the "little and insignificant actions" that other persons might overlook — and the stories in them. They pursue stories to their sources and follow them to their destinations, just as good reporters track down the stories that make the headlines in the daily papers or the feature stories on television.

The storyteller needs a journal in which to record what is seen, lived, and reflected upon from life. Kenneth Heuer, the late Loren Eiseley's editor and friend, writes of him:

Like Thoreau, Eiseley was a journal keeper. If one could have lifted the rooftop of his house in Wynnewood, Pennsylvania, late at night (for he was an insomniac), one would have heard the scratching of his pen or pencil across white sheets of paper in a black-and-red bound legal notebook. The first entry is dated May 21, 1953: "Beginning this journal in my 46th year; a late start for a writer's journal, but I hope to do something with it. During the last few days there have been several nature incidents, and I will try and record them in the hope that they will not thus escape my memory and that I may be able to use them later on."[16]

Heuer mentions that Eiseley kept a daily journal — with some gaps in it — for over two decades, and that:

> *In his journals, Eiseley communed with himself and the world. He set down observations on animals and plants, meditations on man and the universe, and outlines for works he planned to write. Like Thoreau, he drew upon his journals for his articles and books, and many entries found their way into his publications.* [17]

He also recorded data from books he had read — "science, philosophy, literature, theology" — and "in his notebooks he dealt with writers of the past as if they were living. It is almost a communication of great minds." His first book, *The Immense Journey,* is the story of evolution as he perceived the story and recorded much of it in his journal. The preacher who would be a storyteller would do well to follow his example and keep some sort of personal journal of daily observations and thoughts, as most of the great preachers — before and after him — have done. It is important for interesting and pertinent preaching *and* storytelling.

Study the lives and works of great storytellers. Begin with one writer whom you particularly admire, find out what you can about him or her, read what the writer has produced and how it was produced, analyze facts and stories — and learn how to develop your own stories in the process. To become a storyteller, it is necessary to saturate your mind with stories, let them take hold of your imagination through which your stories — fact and fiction — begin to emerge as stories to be told. Some may be small and simple illustrations, others may become story sermons, and still others might be the inspiration for a series of essays or sermons that will proclaim the gospel of the Lord to people as The Story. The great storytellers can help preachers to learn storytelling.

An Introduction to a Great Storyteller

Over half a decade after Loren Eiseley's death, various of his writings are still being published. The cover of *Omni* magazine for June, 1982, after announcing, "Found: Loren Eiseley's Long-Lost Notes on Life, Nature, and the Universe," referred the reader to an article that begins:

Five years after his death, excerpts from the lost journals of one of the twentieth century's greatest naturalists are finally published. One critic has said of him, "If our manic century has produced an heir apparent to Henry David Thoreau, Dr. Eiseley is it." The late Loren Eisely was a man with a rare combination of gifts. He was Benjamin Franklin Professor of Anthropology and the History of Science at the University of Pennsylvania. He has also been acclaimed as one of the finest literary stylists of our time. In 1971 he was elected to the National Institute of Arts and Letters, an honor unique among professional paleontologists, and his book of scientific essays, The Immense Journey, *is now considered a modern classic.*[18]

Heuer, who wrote the introduction to Eiseley's excerpts in the journal, includes only ten of them in the *Omni* issue, which would suggest to me that more of them will appear in book form.

Eiseley was a literary stylist. He produced a half dozen books of poetry, numerous essays and articles, and eight or nine nonfiction books (he rewrote a book on Francis Bacon) including his autobiography, *All the Strange Hours: The Excavation of a Life,* in the twenty years before he died in 1977. His literary genius reached its zenith in the stories he told. He has been called one of the four great storytellers of the twentieth century. He could just be, as more than a few literary critics believe, the greatest storyteller of them all.

What makes Eiseley unique as a storyteller — and a worthwhile model for the preacher — is that, basically he used story to interpret science to people. His stories, for the average reader, first surface as illustrations in the chapters of his books, and some of them are employed as standard methodology; they clarify what he is saying and add interest to his discussions of scientific facts. He never tells a story at the beginning of a chapter without adding other illustrations to keep the readers involved in his thesis or explanation. Here his use of illustration differs radically from those preachers who use a good story at the beginning of the story, gain the attention and interest of the people, but never use any graphic or dramatic story material after the introduction. Eiseley illustrated the entire essay, chapter, or even a book, not merely for the sake of interest but because he would not allow science to remain abstract theory for his readers. He knew that illustration made it concrete as well as clear and interesting.

Loren Eiseley raised the art of illustration to new and higher levels in his writing. In *Reading for Rhetoric,* Caroline Shrodes, Clifford Johnson, and James R. Wilson discuss how Eiseley arranges "Purpose and Structure" in an essay on "The Uncompleted Man." They comment about his unique use of illustration:

> *In this essay, Eiseley is explicit about the ideas he discusses, but the burden of their presentation is carried almost exclusively by illustrations which make the ideas vivid and dramatic as well as immediately comprehensible. Eiseley begins his essay with a reference (illustration) to the witches' scene in Macbeth. He does not state*

the idea he wishes to illustrate until paragraph 3. (a) What are the ideas? (b) What is gained by beginning with the reference to the witches? Why does he not state his ideas and then illustrate them?[19] (emphasis mine).

That he hopes to intrigue his audience with what is to come is obvious, but I suspect that as a teacher he also hopes to get them thinking through — and living — the illustration he puts before their eyes and minds. The preacher would do well to study Loren Eiseley's illustrations and the various methods he invents and employs to enable them to function effectively.

His illustrations should also be studied from the standpoint of story in at least two ways: 1) His stories should be read, analyzed and criticized as models of the art of illustration. He knows how to begin a story, develop the middle section in which encounter takes place in dramatic fashion, incorporate dialogue that is real and relevant to the story and the people in it, use necessary description concisely but beautifully, and end the story in such a way that it leads naturally into a continuing and meaningful discussion of his subject. He also has a range of first-person narrative stories that fit into all of the classifications identified by Richard Thulin. Some are straight *illustrations,* some could be called *reminiscences,* some are clearly *confessions,* but others — and his best — fall into the category of *self-portrayal.* An excellent example of the latter type of first person story-illustration may be found in a chapter of his autobiography *(All the Strange Hours),* titled "A Small Death." He tells the story of the death of a dog in an anatomy laboratory in the University of Kansas (School of Medicine) and how that incident might have changed the course of his life. (He had been invited to attend medical school where he was a teaching assistant in the anatomy laboratory. He turned down the offer and decided to become a naturalist). Several other stories related to the "small death" (the death of a dream — ?) are interwoven masterfully with the main story.

Eiseley's writing became more and more narrative as he approached the end of his career. Two of his last books, *The Night Country* and *All the Strange Hours*, belong together; both are narrative and autobiographical. Eiseley senses that his life is drawing to a close in *The Night Country.* "These chapters, then, are the annals of a long and uncompleted running. I leave them here lest the end come on me unawares as it does upon all fugitives." And he concludes the foreword with this cryptic message:

> *There is a shadow on the wall before me. It is my own; the hour is late. I write in a hotel room at midnight.*
> *Tomorrow the shadow on the wall will be that of another.*[20]

The Night Country is no sentimental journey anymore than it is a sojourn in darkness; in it, Eiseley puts his life into a larger framework — the wonder of the world and life — than if he were merely talking about himself.

Preachers who are interested in doing more first-person narrative preaching in their pulpit ministries would do well to read two chapters of *The Night Country.* Chapter 12 should be read first; it is called "Obituary for a Bone Hunter" and bears strong resemblance to the three-point thematic sermon. He contends that there are two types of "bone hunters" — archeologists and anthropologists — the "big bone hunters" who have made no important "finds" during their careers. He calls himself a "small bone hunter" and tells the stories of three missed opportunities — involving spiders, an egg, and a "madman" — to become a "big bone hunter." He finishes the stories on a note of resignation:

> *Thirty years have passed since the old man came to see me. I have crawled in many caverns, stooped with infinte aching patience over the bones of many men. I have made no discoveries.*
>
> *I think how that in some strange way that old man out of the autumn leaf was the last test of the inscrutable gods. There will be no further chances. The egg and the spiders and the mad-man — in them is the obituary of a life dedicated to the folly of doubt, the life of a small bone hunter.*[21]

His message to the reader is intended to be more than missed opportunities on this part, but the reader must find the message with further help. Some might be motivated to recognize — and take advantage of — opportunities to learn, to grow, to serve, and to live life to its fullest in an "you only go around once" kind of existence.

Chapter 11, "One Night's Dying," should be read after "Obituary for a Bone Hunter" — from a narrative preaching perspective. It tells a different story and in a different way. "One Night's Dying" relates how Eiseley became an insomniac after his father died a long and painful death, and how as he gave up on sleep and tried to read, his grandmother came and sat with him:

> *My grandmother saw the light burning through the curtains of my door and came to sit with me. A few years later, when I touched her hair in farewell at the beginning of a journey from which I would not return to see her alive, I knew*

she had saved my sanity. Into that lonely room at midnight she had come, abandoning her own sleep, in order to sit with one in trouble. We had not spoken much, but we had sat together by the lamp, reasserting our common humanity before the great empty dark that is the universe. [22]

His grandmother did not reestablish his sleep pattern, but more importantly, "she had brought me out of a dark room and retied my thread of life to the living world. Henceforth, by night or day . . . I have not been able merely to endure but to make the best of what many regard as an unbearable affliction." [23]

The rest of the story is about how his fear of death, which he believes brought on his insomnia — "deep-seated in my subconscious is the gateway to the tomb" — found resolution in his life, especially in two connected incidents. The first happened in his dimly lit study when a firefly appeared and flew from book to book, making an extended landing on one book before it flew off; Eiseley went over, picked it up, opened it at random and relates: "I came immediately upon these words from St. Paul: 'Beareth all things, believeth all things, hopeth all things, endureth all things.' " The second incident followed immediately with this invitation: "In this final episode I shall ask you to bear with me and also to believe."

Eiseley proceeds to tell about a mystical experience he had after missing a plane in a foreign city. As he sat in a nearly deserted airport, a man came toward him, "limping painfully and grotesquely upon a heavy cane." He tried to put the man out of his mind but ". . . the man limped on relentlessly" toward him. Eiseley:

How, oh God, I entreated, did we become entrapped within this substance out of which we stare so helplessly upon our own eventual dissolution? How for a single minute could we dream or imagine that thought would save us, children deliver us, from the body of death?[24] *(emphasis mine)*

The man came close enough that Eiseley could smell a deathlike odor, but he didn't draw back from the man because "I had lived with death too many years":

And then this strange thing happened, which I do not mean physically and cannot explain. The man entered me. From that moment I saw him no more. For a moment I was contorted within his shape, and then out of his body — our bodies, rather — there arose some inexplicable sweetness of union, some understanding between body and spirit which I had never before experienced . . .

As I went toward my plane (some time later) the words the firefly had found for me came automatically to my lips. "Beareth all things," believe, believe. It is thus that one night's dying becomes tomorrow's birth. I, who do not sleep, can tell you this.[25]

The conclusion to this story-chapter in *The Night Country* is almost sermonic — "believe, believe" — and the reader is left with the impression that this Jacob- at-the-Jabbok-like experience resolved his fear of death and the tomb. "One Night's Dying" reads like "a story told" — by a scientist instead of a preacher. (It is offered for its style, not gospel content.)

Some conclusions, which apply to the business of sermon illustration and, particularly, to the biblical narrative sermon, may be drawn from these two examples from the same book. A more extensive study of his writings and techniques would substantiate them and make additional contributions to our knowledge of the essential function of illustration in the sermon and narrative shapes for the sermon.

First, Eiseley's works demonstrate the importance of the central idea, or what Richard Caemmerer might term the topic, in a story or, for us, a sermon. H. Grady Davis called it the "generative idea" or the story-idea.

Second, Eiseley is cognizant of the fact that storytelling, as a difficult art, calls for a radically new idea for shaping the plot of each story. His chapter-stories, as in "Obituary for a Bone Hunter" and "One Night's Dying" and others, reflect his concern for finding forms for his stories and exposition that will assist the reader to "fashion these thoughts within himself."

Third, Eiseley has developed the sense of perception, which is so crucial in the kind of writing he does and in preaching, too, to a very high degree. Read, for example, "The Last Magician" in *The Invisible Pyramid.*

Fourth, Eiseley is the embodiment of the Renaissance Man in that he was well read in literature, philosophy, medicine, poetry, drama, theology, and science, but the first-person narrative illustrations and stories are the most powerful materials in his books. He is a storyteller *par excellence.*

Fifth, he has also written some of the most vivid parables in the English language, and these constitute a study in themselves. The well-known "Judgment of the Birds" parables (three) in *The Immense Journey* help to make the book memorable. The posthumously-published *The Star Thrower,* which he had prepared and named before his death, is titled after what some believe is his greatest parable when it first appeared in *The Unexpected Universe.* Others include: "The Innocent Fox," "The Last Magician," "The Strangeness in the Proportion." Preachers will benefit immeasurably through a study of these parables.

Loren Eiseley once entered a crowded railroad car in New York City and made his way to the only empty seat which was next to a giant of a man, who was slouched down as though he were drunk. He seemed to be asleep — until the conducter came to collect the tickets and then he "straightened up, whipped out his ticket and took on a sharp alertness . . . When the conductor was gone the big man turned to me with a glimmer of amusement in his eyes. 'Stranger,' he appealed before I could return to my book, 'tell me a story.' " Eiseley seems to have heard that request from the people in the world who were likely to read his books — "Tell us a story." He did just that.

A cursory reading of some of his works will fortify the preacher with a stock of illustrations that might be used in various kinds of sermons. But a careful reading of them, plus a study of his narrative story-chapters in many of the books, will assist the preacher not only in mastering the art of sermon illustration but also in learning how to plan and construct various kinds of story sermons. Eiseley, almost more than any other writer — secular or clergy — can help the preacher to become a storyteller so that in biblical story sermons, particularly, the preacher may tell The Story.

7 Telling the Sermon

The Cathedral of St. John Lateran in Rome, the principal if not the best-known church of Roman Catholicism, is a place that excites one's imagination. It is inextricably connected to the rise of Christianity in the West; it is not simply an edifice of architectural significance but a complex of buildings where history was made. Volumes of stories — some dramatically compelling and others rather revolting — could be, and have been, written about St. John Lateran. It has evolved since the fourth century from a palace to a church to a cathedral to which was added, in time, a baptistry for the city of Rome. It is the church, the cathedral, that makes a statement about preaching to us.

This great church is dedicated to Christ "and in honor of St. John the Baptist and St. John the Evangelist, " but it also honors all of the Apostles. The heads of Peter and Paul are reputed to be in a marble tabernacle, but there are great statues of the Apostles surrounding the nave of the church. "Within (the nave), the spaciousness and majesty, the splendour of marble, the cosmatesque floor, and the statues of the Apostles erect in their tabernacles which face one another from two rows of great pillars, at once make themselves felt."[1] These statues stand there as if each is waiting for an opportunity to tell the story of his experiences with the Christ and the stories of the struggle in proclaiming the gospel. One could wish that, instead of standing there as silent witnesses, they could be transformed into the kinds of figures in the Hall of Presidents in Disneyworld and given voices so that they could actually speak out and tell The Story in their own words. It could be a lesson for preachers in "telling their sermons" within the worship of God's people.

Sermons, Like Stories, Should Be Told

Good storytellers *tell* their stories; they don't read them, because stories are meant to be told. Richard Jensen reminds us:

> *Storytelling . . . is also composed of some basic ingredients that we recognize as somewhat obvious when we hear them set forth. Storytelling, for example, should be done freely and spontaneously.* **Stories should not be read nor should they bear the marks of a kind of wooden memorization process.** *(emphasis mine) The words we use and the way we use them with the marvelous instrument of the human voice are the most important ingredients in the art of storytelling.*[2]

And, he adds, "Our facial expressions, the movement of our eyes (the focal point of the listener's gaze) and the gestures of our hands are also important aspects of this act." The whole person needs to be involved in the telling of stories.

Jensen also believes that sermons should be told, not

read to the people, especially any type of story sermon. The delivery should complement the style of the sermon, thus the story sermon should be delivered in the manner of the storyteller. Extend the image of the *storyteller* far enough and apply it to the preacher rather than the traditional image of *herald*, as Edmund Steimle suggests, and it applies to the delivery of the sermon as well as its content and form. Jensen understands this connection between the sermon and its delivery better than most of the other persons writing about the story sermon, or the sermon in general. Thor Hall, another systematician who believes that the sermon should be spoken naturally by most preachers, was concerned with the language of the sermon but not with the way the sermon is shaped. Theological jargon and God-talk, in his opinion, need to give way to "believing God-talk" that communicates to people with vivid imagery:

> *Believing God-talk does not function as a mighty rocket with a capsule full of sensitive instruments that is shot off to some distant spot in the universe, there to hit its transcendent target and send reliable information back to earth. Rather, this language represents the limited thrust that sends aloft little packages of earthly fireworks, which when they explode in the night, tell all who see it that there is a celebration of some sort. Somebody is festive, and they have something to tell (emphasis mine). Something has happened to them, and from the color of their fireworks it must be something wonderful.*[3]

Story is implicit in Hall's description of the language of the sermon, but it never becomes explicit in *The Future Shape of Preaching*. He seems to be talking about good communication — and in the service of worship — but not about "telling the Story" as Jensen does.

Richard Lischer is the third systematician to press preachers to preach with freedom from the manuscript *because*, he emphasizes, preaching is an *oral* event. The recovery of its orality by preachers in their preaching is, for him, a theological as well as practical necessity. Lischer calls the Epistles and Gospels a "frozen record of oral discourse," declaring, "Perhaps no one understood the oral nature of the Christian message better than Luther, who claimed somewhere that the Gospel should not be written but screamed, and promulgated a confessional definition of the gospel that totally bypassed its written character."[4] Lischer reminds us that Luther preached his sermons rather in the manner of the apostles, his models: "Of the apostles, he said, 'Before they wrote, they first of all preached to the people by word of mouth and converted them, and this was their real apostolic and New Testament work.' " Luther considered their "need to write books a serious decline and a lack of the Spirit which necessity forced upon us; it is not the real manner of the New Testament."[5] He really abandoned writing out his sermons sometime after he published his *Church Postils,* not simply because he was pressed for time, but because he wanted to keep the sermon in oral form. Most of his published sermons subsequently are reports of what students and friends heard him say when he preached. He understood that preaching is "telling the Story."

Lischer scores contemporary preaching quite severely from the perspective of oral communication of the gospel and insists that preaching "needs to set its own house in order" by taking seriously the delivery of the sermon:

So debased is preaching as an oral event that manuscripts are called sermons, and in some places seminarians are taught to preach by being made to read their manuscripts (in preaching labs). And what we know of the gifted preachers, we too often discover via printed collections of the year's "best" sermons, usually selected according to non-oral non-homiletical criteria, such as the writer's academic respectability, poeticality of expression, or ecclesiastical reputation.[6]

And Lischer notes that "rallying people around the Word" in public worship is similarly affected:

As if the loss of authentic orality — by means of literary manuscript preaching, slide shows, liturgists in leotards and similar events — were not bad enough, now many churches are distributing printed copies of the scriptural lessons for the day, so that when the lector says, "Hear the Word of God." the congregation in a single movement buries its nose in the bulletin.[7]

Lischer's main point in his observations and arguments for recovering the orality of preaching is that one of the ways the preaching serves theology is by helping theology — through the proclamation of the gospel — recover *its* oral character. Without showing how content and sermon shape contribute to the oral character of preaching, both Richard Lischer and Thor Hall, among others, are talking about what has been called "preaching without notes." "Telling the Story" surpasses that theory because it combines content and sermon shape so as to make the sermon event a telling of the Story in the context of worship.

The Manuscript as a Homiletical Hang-up

Numerous neophyte preachers in the seminaries,

when confronted by a videotape playback of their first sermons, remark, "I had no idea that I was looking at my manuscript so much of the time," or "I didn't realize how much my head was bobbing up and down," or "I looked lifeless in the pulpit, didn't I?" Closed circuit television impresses upon them the importance of pulpit communication that is genuinely oral in character. It underlines the importance of sermon delivery in which visual, verbal, and body communication may be established and maintained with the people.[8] This translates into preaching without notes, which is another way of saying that for many students, the sermon must be thoroughly learned after it is constructed. "I'll be fortunate to have sufficient time to prepare my sermons as they should be prepared, won't I? How will I ever find time to learn them with all the other facets of ministry that demand attention?" are their honest, nondefensive questions. The answer to these questions is more involved than how to find time to prepare and learn the sermon so that it may be preached without notes or with a minimal use of notes (outline) in the pulpit.

The preacher's theological understanding of preaching and his or her attitude toward the pulpit ministry constitute one problem area that has ramifications for sermon delivery. Nearly everyone who goes to church knows a preacher who is able to tell story after story in a social gathering — and may be the very life of the party — but is a totally different person in the pulpit. There the preacher becomes a *reader* whose personality is inhibited, whose thought processes are restricted, and whose "pulpit power" is seriously diminished. In a social setting, the person communicates orally, but in the pulpit the preacher's performance is more literary than oral. Decades ago Andrew W. Blackwood analyzed this sort of preacher as one who "seems to be setting up three hurdles such as few men can clear successfully Sunday" in the pulpit:

1. I have here a message so masterly that I must present it exactly in this form.

2. I have written with such artistry that I must call attention to my literary prowess.

3. I can read with such skill that no one will dream I am reading.[9]

Blackwood says that the first hurdle sounds like a claim of "verbal inspiration" to a "disbeliever in the method." Of the second, he asks, "Who can produce a masterpiece of literature every week?" And of the third hurdle, he contends that "only an exceptional minister can preach this way without calling attention to himself and his powers."[10] The homiletician who is concerned about content, form, and delivery of the sermon has heard all three of these arguments from pastors as well as students. The most difficult method of delivering the sermon with effectiveness is by reading the manuscript exactly as it has been prepared.

The list of reasons why preachers read their sermons might be expanded indefinitely; some preachers seem to be too timid to get away from their manuscripts, others are not convinced that an oral speaking style is really necessary considering the amount of time it takes to learn a sermon, and more than a few argue that the skill involved demands too high a price for the preacher. And it is evident to every teacher of homiletics that there are a few people who must rely on their manuscripts when delivering their sermons, but certainly not as many as actually are "bound to the script." There are skills to be learned in connection with sermon delivery — and most preachers can learn them. Some of them involve mental as well as physical effort to attain proficiency in an oral style. One must develop the imagination to some extent; this is easily done with the memorization of dialogue, quotations, Scripture passages, and even portions of Psalms and liturgical prayers. The preacher who develops the sermon plan, or outline, in logical fashion and is able to memorize it is but a short step away from preaching without notes. Equally important to the use of one's memory and learning how to use voice, have eye contact, and develop a style of speaking that Blackwood called "animated conversation," is the manner in which the manuscript is planned and prepared. The style of the manuscript itself may be the biggest hurdle of all to a natural and effective style of delivery in the pulpit.

Story and the Mastery of the Manuscript

The shape, or style, of the sermon either assists or hinders the preacher in the delivery of the sermon. The manuscript itself must contribute to the final step in the homiletical process, the preaching of the gospel. Time and again I write at the bottom of "critic sheets" after playback and discussion of a sermon in preaching lab, "Learn a method of preparing the manuscript so that you can preach without reading it verbatim or referring constantly to it." Many students seem to have adopted "models" who read their sermons to their people, but the problem is deeper than that; it has to do with the style of the sermons that are being preached. The only way that many sermons can be preached in anything resembling oral style is by memorizing them. Homileticians from Andrew Blackwood, in the 1940's and 50s, to Clyde Fant, as recently as 1975, have discarded this approach to competent sermon delivery. A manuscript has to be done in an oral style.

Another of the contributions that Grady Davis made to homiletics was his concept of "Writing for the

Ear."[12] He taught that different types of words and sentences need to be used in speaking than in writing; he was urging preachers to think *orally* as they write their sermons. Fant was aware that homileticians had long been advising students and preachers to develop their manuscripts in an oral style but that oral style has remained elusive. He suggests a method of sermon preparation which he calls "the oral manuscript," as a replacement for the written manuscript. He begins with exegetical study of the text and pastoral reflection to focus upon the sermon theme and thrust, followed by a preliminary plan. Up to this point, thought has been central to the sermon preparation, but from this point on, Fant declares, it is a *matter of speech.*

After writing the "tentative divisions" of the sermon theme on a sheet of paper, he suggests a "rough oral draft" that is developed by speech:

> *Then preach aloud on each of them as long as ideas suggest themselves, using free association. Make no effort to hinder the free flow of ideas or to arrange them in order at this time. But keep a pen in hand and pause in speaking only long enough to note briefly the key directional phrases or sentences that emerge.*[13]

This involves "thought-blocks"[14] as in the written sermon — "except that it is being done in the medium which will eventually be used." Because the preacher can hear what is being said, not just look at words on a page, the preacher is able to evaluate the thought, the structure, and the movement of the sermon, so that the basic content is set. From the experience of attempting to speak the sermon, the preacher is prepared to revise it, preach it aloud once more, and then do *the final draft of the oral manuscript.* A "sermon brief" — not a sermon outline nor a written manuscript — is the end result of this process.[15]

I have no doubt that this approach to developing the oral quality of the sermon may be effective, but it does not automatically alter the shape of the sermon; it is not "writing for the ear" since the written manuscript is omitted altogether in the preparation of the sermon. The so-called *sermon brief* might become very detailed, approximating a written sermon — and if it becomes detailed as is implicit in Fant's example,[16] the preacher could have a major memorization problem at hand. I suggest that neither Davis' "writing for the ear" nor Fant's "oral manuscript" will necessarily change the style of the sermon to the extent requisite for effective oral communication in the pulpit. Preachers need to learn to *write for the mouth* — not merely for the ear or not writing at ail — and this is where story takes over.

Some forty years ago, Clarence E. Macartney, renowned minister of First Presbyterian Church, Pittsburgh, Pennsylvania, published some lectures he had given at Princeton Seminary in a book titled *Preaching Without Notes.* Of sermon delivery he said, "Every consecrated man in the ministry strives to preach in the most effective way . . . The question is: What method of preaching is likely to do the most good?" Macartney was not concerned with preaching good sermons or being called a "good preacher" but with "sermons that will do good." He answers his own question this way: "There can be no question that the sermon that does the most good is the sermon which is preached without notes."[17] How the sermon is delivered is critical because the message is communicated and heard through the words that the preacher speaks. Macartney is not downplaying the content of the sermon when he says this as though the preacher's presence and personality in the pulpit are all that matter; his is not a "medium is the message" conception of oral communication in preaching. He firmly believed that the Word is the message and that the preacher is the messenger.

When Macartney talks about "preaching without notes," he is really speaking about the content of the sermon and how it is arranged so that the speaker may readily preach it without reading it to the people. He does devote one chapter of his book to the discussion of its theme, "Preaching without notes," and he warns that "preaching without notes is by all the hardest way (to deliver a sermon), both as to preparation and delivery." It does not eliminate the arduous business of writing the sermon. Strangely enough, only this one chapter in the book is directly related to the title and the theme of the book; the rest of the book has to do with content and related matters. Macartney's real concern was for biblical preaching, and preaching without notes is the biblical way to preach the good news. And although he believes that there may be some value in the reading of sermons and, he says that "it may be used by the Holy Spirit to save a soul from death (but) it is never preaching in the highest sense." He asks:

Who could picture Jesus reading the Sermon on the Mount or the parable of the Good Samaritan, or the story of the lost son, or of the lost sheep? Who could think of him reading his sevenfold denunciation of the scribes and Pharisees? Who could think of Paul reading his sermon to the philosophers on Mars Hill, or even turning aside to consult notes in his hand as he spoke? Who could think of Paul standing on the seashore at Miletus and reading to the elders of the church at Ephesus his beautiful valedictory address? Who could think of Peter on the day of Pentecost pulling out a manuscript and reading the divine summons to repent and believe on the Lord Jesus Christ?[18]

In his opinion, therefore, "reading a sermon, however profitable and well done it may be, is not in reality preaching at all." Preaching without notes, he argues, is biblical preaching. The shape of the content, which he discovered in the Bible, is what makes preaching without notes a possibility for the average parish preacher; Macartney had discovered that the Bible as story could be — had to be — *told, not read,* to the people. I believe he had discovered that story is what makes preaching without notes a viable reality for almost every preacher. That's why most of the book is concerned with content and "other matters," and particularly with sermon illustration which, to him, meant story. The preacher learns to master the manuscript in the pulpit — or preach without notes, as Macartney puts it — through the use of story. The "mechanics" [19] of such preaching are important, of course, but story is the real secret of learning to preach without notes, or to preach biblically.

Story and Sermon Delivery

When the content and shape of the sermon are informed by — and take the shape of — story, Macartney's type of *biblical delivery* — without any notes or extensive use of notes — is attainable in preaching. Telling The Story begins in the Bible itself, Macartney advised:

> *The preacher who is going to preach for the first time without notes would do well to start with Bible biography or use the Bible stories. These themes give him something easy to remember. There is always a certain advantage in preaching on the great characters and the* great *narratives of the Bible.* [20] (emphasis mine)

Macartney recognized that such subject matter was relatively easy to preach without notes because that was the natural manner by which to proclaim it. From the Bible he learned that *"any story is always better told than read"* (italics mine). He also discovered the twofold nature of the biblical story and offered it to preachers: "When one tells a story from the Bible, or bases a story (sermon) on the life of a Bible character, he will find plenty of illustration in the story itself." The Story, the larger stories or pericopes, and the little stories — or illustrations — are the key to finding a format for the sermon that facilitates "mastery of the manuscript" by preachers. Illustration is especially helpful, ever essential, in learning how to preach without notes, according to Macartney's treatment of the subject in his book.

Arndt Halvorson, one of my colleagues in homiletics, and I discovered, as we were discussing story and sermon delivery one day, that both of us learned to preach without notes largely by the use of story and illustration in the sermon. We learned the importance of story — and we learned how to tell stories. But before we began to make extensive use of story and illustration in our sermons, we had some difficulty in learning how to preach without notes; we found it difficult to remember some of our sermons. Each of us had tried the memorization route to sermon delivery, and rejected it because — for different reasons — it didn't work. We learned independently of each other — and of Macartney — that story is of critical importance to preaching with freedom from one's notes. Macartney was absolutely right, in our opinion, when he declared that "sermons which are based on life and life's experiences not only hold a congregation but lend themselves to free presentation on the part of the preacher without the need of a manuscript."[21] Such sermons can be like "a story told" in the delivery as well as in content. Content, shape, and delivery complement each other — and preaching may become holistic when preachers recognize this relationship and allow story to inform their preaching.

Illustration, as a paragraph-length story, affords the preacher the opportunity to learn how to preach at least part of the sermon without notes. If the preacher accepts the assertion that good stories need to be told to be as fully effective as they can be, he or she is on a course that could lead to preaching the entire sermon without any manuscript. And so, the preacher should learn stories used as illustration, memorizing details of plot and dialogue by following Clyde Fant's "oral manuscript" — or speaking — method. The importance of dialogue over description needs to be ascertained before the preacher is likely to make any concerted effort to learn the dialogue of a story so that it can be delivered with force and conviction in the sermon. When preachers are able to *tell* their illustrations, they have taken a big step toward telling the entire sermon when they preach. They develop confidence in their preaching ability that encourages them to attempt to preach without any notes at all. The mastery of the art of illustration can help preachers get "out of the Gutenberg galaxy," as Clyde Fant tags the reading of a manuscript in the pulpit.

Story sermons of the type advocated by Richard Jensen and Charles Rice (and others) are extremely useful in helping preachers make the transition from telling part of a sermon — the illustrations — to preaching the whole sermon in a narrative style. They resemble an illustration that has been expanded from a brief story to a longer one. Both may have:

A beginning which gets us directly acquainted with the people and the setting, a stating of the problem (or plot), the action that carried that

*plot along toward its climax and a quick move-
ment toward the conclusion: that's one way to
describe the basic structure of a story . . .*[22]

Since it is also the basic structure of the story sermon,
learning the whole sermon is quite similar to learning a
long illustration or a short story. This format simplifies
the process of mastering the manuscript so that the
sermon can be told by the preacher. If for no other
reason than to improve one's delivery, this type of story
sermon ought to be attempted a few times. And if the
preacher does tell the sermon with freedom and
spontaneity, the people are likely to respond with
enthusiasm, "That sermon really reached me today,
Pastor."

The Steimle-Niedenthal-Rice type of biblical
sermon is a bit more complicated as far as learning it and
delivering it without notes are concerned. But when the
preacher learns to develop the sermon by following the
story line of the gospel pericope, the task is considerably
simplified. Familiarity with the biblical story at hand
means that the preacher is working within a framework
that builds up confidence and self-assurance for telling
the story. It might be well to begin with simple biblical
narratives, as Macartney suggests, and then move into
the more complicated, but still easily learned, "a story
told" kind of story sermon. Telling the sermon in the
setting of worship will contribute to the edification of
the people of God as they sing their song of praise and
thanksgiving. Only then will preaching become holistic,
or liturgical, preaching.

The secret, if there is one, in preaching as if one were
telling a story is in *rethinking the story sermon* as it is
being preached. This involves some memorization: plot
or outline of the sermon, key sentences, dialogue, and
similar details including the introduction and the
conclusion. Story helps in this process — personal

experiences and familiar Bible stories that have meant much to the preacher — because the preacher may relive them as they are being told in the sermon, and this remembering and reliving of the story material helps the preacher to rethink the story sermon that was prepared with care and perception as it is being preached. Preachers who are wiling to attempt this holistic method of preaching will discover that it is a method that most pastors can learn and master. And when they have gained some skill at preaching story sermons this way, their congregations will insist that they never give it up because preaching will really be a significant event that inspires the song the people sing.

8 Solving the Story Problems

It has been many years since I first read Thomas Chalmers' famous sermon, "The Expulsive Power of a New Affection." Until recently, it was one of the almost universally-studied sermons in theological schools, largely because of Chalmers structure and style. It ought to be studied today — not for matters of language and form — but for its origin. The story behind it is what makes it interesting and pertinent to contemporary story preaching. It reveals one of the essential factors in solving the "story problems" that most preachers seem to face today: how to find a sufficient supply of illustrations and stories for their sermons.

Chalmers often made the trip from Edinburgh, Scotland, to Glasgow by horse-drawn coach. He liked to sit up on top of the coach beside the driver, and he rode up there as often as possible. He noticed that one particular driver always flicked his whip at one of the horses; it was always the same horse and always at the same place in the road. Finally, he asked the driver why he did this and received an explanation from the man. It seems that the horse in question was afraid of something real or imaginery that inhabited that spot in the highway. He would balk, even rear on occasion, and throw off the even gait of the team. When the driver realized why this was happening, he diverted the horses's attention from what frightened him by nipping him sharply with his whip, and the horse would immediately settle down and quickly resume the correct pace. Chalmers realized that the introduction of a new factor into the situation freed the horse from the influence of whatever disturbed and frightened him at that point in the trip. This gave him the idea for a sermon meant to edify his hearers by showing them that the only way that our love of the world can be expelled from the heart is through the expulsive power of a new affection which, for the Christian, is the love of the Father. The text for the sermon was 1 John 2:15 — "Love not the world, neither the things that are in the world. If any man love the world, the love of the Father is not in him." The story of the horse and driver does not surface in the sermon but the sermon would not have been conceived without the combination of text and story.

Chalmers was in touch with life, and that was one of the reasons that he was a great preacher. He observed what was happening, investigated what he saw and heard, and reflected — with perception — on matters that to others might seem insignificant. Were he living and preaching today, there is no doubt in my mind that the style of his sermons would be different; he would tell more of what he had seen and experienced in incidents like that of the driver who touched his whip to one of his horses to regain his attention to the task in which he was engaged. I suspect that Thomas Chalmers would tell The Story and that he would have an almost unlimited supply of illustrations to interweave with the gospel story.

The Illustration-Story Problem

To preach biblical story sermons — or any other kind of sermon that is concrete and narrative in character — requires that the preacher have a veritable storehouse of sermon resources. Graphic sermons literally consume illustrations and stories to such a degree that the preacher never seems to have enough of them. For too many preachers who understand the importance of illustration-story in the sermon — and who never seem to have the stories and anecdotes they need — Friday is, apparently, crucial to the homiletical process, and the search for illustrative matter turns what might be an orderly procedure for building the sermon into a "homiletical crash program." And preachers have told me that when they work that way, the real crash occurs on Sunday morning. Their illustrations are either limited in number and often are insufficient in quality and theme for the task they should perform in the sermon. Preachers say that they need help in finding illustrations and stories for their sermons.

A current writing assignment to do some "preaching helps" for a journal used ecumenically includes, among the instructions for completing the task, this suggestion: "If possible, include at least one story. Subscribers are clamoring for stories . . . At least half the material should be *original:* stories, thoughts, examples, odd connections, reminiscences, applications, etc., out of your own experience . . . Err on the side of the simple and the homely, rather than the elegant and the eloquent . . ." Arndt Halvorson is aware of the demand for stories and illustrative material and comments:

> *An eavesdropper on a group of preachers in informal discussion could well wonder if . . . concern with the text is shared by all. In their un-guarded moment, preachers seem more con-*

cerned with getting what they call "preaching ideas." They ask, "Have you read any good books lately?" They ask, "Have you heard any good illustrations?" They ask, "What do you think of the latest television preacher?" Resisting the impulse to moralize about such apparent lack of concern for biblical scholarship and theological issues, we can recognize that preachers are concerned that their sermons be interesting, contemporary, stimulating. They feel the pressure of being heard. [1]

And they know what parts of the sermon people really hear, thus their continuing concern with the accumulation of usable stories for their own preaching ministry. The real problem is that, for maximum effectiveness in sermon preparation and genuine impact in their sermons, they ought to find their own materials. Time and know-how appear to be at the heart of the problem.

Attuned as they are to their market among the parish pastors, publication houses respond with the publication of sermons that pick up where Martin Luther left off in his *Church Postils* (from *post illa verba,* "after the word"). The function is to assist preachers in rounding out their sermons so that they will be holistic from a theological, biblical, and pastoral perspective. They are intended to be resources for preaching — "helps" — and not necessarily sermonic models. Those who oppose the publication of entire sermon manuscripts do so, I am told, because preachers tend to bypass the intention of writers and publishers by culling out the illustrations for their sermons and, more or less, discarding the rest of the sermons except, it is claimed, "for an occasional idea." "Why not," some of these critics ask, "stop publishing sermons?"

Some sermon "helps" do concentrate on the

circulation of illustrations and stories among the preachers who subscribe to their service, leaving it up to the preacher to accept or reject them, to use or not use them — as they choose — in their sermons. They believe it to be entirely legitimate to incorporate some other person's stories in their sermons; after all, almost every preacher has done this at one time or other in his or her ministry. When sources are given and the stories behind the stories are printed, too, the publication of illustrative sermon materials takes on additional significance. The readers are encouraged to mine other stories from the sources and to adopt as their own methods that will enable them to discover their own illustrations and stories. Preachers learn about preaching from other preachers. Modern versions of the *Church Postils* are important because they teach preachers how to incorporate illustrations into their sermons instead of merely offering stories to the preachers.

When it was first published, I found Leslie Waterhead's *When the Lamp Flickers*[2] to be a fascinating volume of sermons for homiletical study. It was apparent why Weatherhead could fill the City Temple in London so that his sermons had to be piped into overflow rooms — even after he retired and was over eighty years of age. Weatherhead's sermons proved him to be in touch with the Bible, on the one hand, and with life, on the other. He knew the art of sermon illustration *as it related to pastoral preaching.* Some readers only discovered stories and illustrations in his sermons, but those who studied them uncovered their true worth and the power of Weatherhead's pulpit ministry in his use of experience, memory, and imagination in narrative material, his pastoral concern for the health and spiritual growth of his congregation, his skill in planning and producing consistently effective sermons, and his scholarship in biblical and theological matters. To study sermons like his — in other preachers, too — is continuing education in homiletics.

But sermons, like the Bible, ought to be read and allowed to speak for themselves. Do the words printed on the page come alive as you read them? Do they "speak" (is the style really oral)? Do the stories demand to be told *again* — by you and others? Does the sermon hold your attention all the way to the conclusion? Questions like these need to be asked and answered by a simple "why" and "how?" How does the preacher move from text to sermon? How does the preacher develop the theme — and the story line — of the message? Why? Why does the preacher use the style employed in any given sermon? Why does the preacher do theology — or not do it — this way? Why does the preacher preach this type of sermon in the worship setting? How does this sermon relate to the sacraments and the sacramental life of the people? Sermons, you see, allow readers to ask questions of them that would not be asked when illustrations alone are read by the preachers. This makes them, in my opinion, more valuable than "bare" stories or collections of illustrations. And depending on one's choice of preachers, the reader may engage in sermon study that will contribute in mastering the biblical-narrative sermon style.

Resources for Preaching

Eyes and ears — and a perceptive mind — are the preacher's most important assets for discovering sermon resources in the shape of stories and illustrations. Without developing perception for seeing, hearing, and reflecting upon what happens around them, preachers are reduced to buying books of illustrations, subscribing to the several types of "sermon helps" on the market, reading volumes of sermons, and collecting stories from whatever reading programs they have developed — or their hunt-for-illustrations procedures. Perception enables preachers to recognize the implications and the consequences of what is seen and heard; not merely what is observed and overheard. It identifies the important stories that occur as everyday, or accidental, occurrences, and assists preachers in discerning the theological implications in them.

In a chapter of his *Authentic Preaching,* Arndt Halvorson writes about "Our Hidden Resources" — how they may be found in our parishioners, in the world around us, and in literature. The latter helps us to find the language for preaching effectively and to understand the human situation.[3] Of Flannery O'Connor, he says, "Her writings encourage us never to let up in our explorations of solid biblical theology."[4] He also states:

> *I also want to encourage you to use more wisely the literary resources of our own age. Every preacher, I believe, should find rich mines of insight — theological and human — from reading Franz Kafka, William Golding, Morris West, John Updike, Hermann Hesse, Saul Bellow, Chaim Potok — to mention a few.*
>
> *There are writers like Frederick Buechner and Loren Eiseley whose works are in a special way helpful to preachers.[5]*

He asserts that Elie Wiesel "is seeking a center for a centerless age," and observes that the great novelists (Steinbeck, Hemingway, Faulkner, Joyce, Fitzgerald, and others) "don't explicitly concern themselves with theological questions, neither do they ignore them. They probe what we call the human situation."

Theology surfaces in many books that have been called minor classics, such as Peter Mattheissen's *At*

Play in the Fields of the Lord, Ray Bradbury's *The Martian Chronicles,* or Antoine de Saint Exupery's *Wind, Sand and Stars.* For example, "St. X" writes about his crash in the Libyan desert as his plane went down, lost in the night. He and his mechanic survived, walked across the sands for five days before — almost dead — they were rescued by a Bedouin. He recorded the experience after he awakened between white sheets — and then spelled out what it meant to him in two theologically perceptive reveries. He wrote of water as "not necessary to life, but life itself," and of the Bedouin as a kind of Christ figure:

> *You, Bedouin of Libya, who saved our lives, though you will dwell forever in my memory yet I shall never be able to recapture your features. You are Humanity and your face comes into my mind simply as man incarnate. You, our beloved fellowman, did not know whom we might be, and yet you recognized us without fail. And I, in my turn, shall recognize you in the faces of all mankind. You came towards me in an aureole of charity and magnanimity bearing the gift of water. All my friends and all my enemies marched toward me in your person.* It did not seem to me that you were rescuing me; rather did it seem that you were forgiving me. And I felt I had no enemy left in all the world.[6] (emphasis mine)

Isn't that close to what we are trying to convey to people when we preach about his body broken and his blood shed "for many for the forgiveness of sins"? Shouldn't our experience of his forgiveness be something like that when the Word is preached, confession made, absolution offered, and the meal partaken? It has been said that the classics (and near-classics, we might add) often contain more theology in them than the sermons preached in our pulpits. By reading them with perception, and over against the Bible and the theological framework within which we preach, this can be corrected as it should be — and within the aegis of story and the narrative-biblical sermon. A good and regular reading program may be most helpful in developing the kind of perception we need to preach the gospel to people today.

Connecting the Classics to Contemporary Life

Television offers preachers another important resource for discovering stories and illustrative materials which might be useful in the preaching ministry as it concerns story sermons. I have heard preachers say that they are reticent to incorporate illustrations from television programs lest their members conclude that they are spending too much time in front of the TV set. It has been said that one would have to be almost mindless to watch television without discrimination: much of it is worthless to most of us. But many people spend hours viewing television; it is an invaluable companion for the lonely and the persons confined to their homes or beds. It is one of the most powerful forces at work in the shaping of values and styles of living of the people who come to church on Sunday. One unnamed commentator went so far as to say that "Television will determine the kind of people that we are." In a book that every preacher ought to read, Neil Postman insists that "television is the primary curriculum" for most people living today. He shows how children are affected by it, and other studies have reached conclusions similar to his; even the commercials on television are "real" to children — part of the program itself. *Teaching as a Conserving Activity,* Postman believes (and so titles his book) is a possibility in our educational system, but only when the impact of television is comprehended and allowed to inform the teacher how to speak and teach. If preaching, too, is conceived to be "a conserving activity," our pastors had better learn why people watch so much television *and* why it has such a powerful effect on them.

Television can — and does — affect people positively and, in some ways, for the better. It makes clear to us exactly what the world around us is like through news programs, specials, and documentaries. A few hours of television viewing a week can enable us to see what life is like all over the world. People have *seen* hunger, the tragedy of war, the plight of the homeless — whether victims of natural catastrophies or human actions — and they have *seen — not just heard about —* joyous events in the life of people and nations. They know about the effects of acid rain, PCBs, ICBMs, terrorism, medicine, psychology, scientific research, space probes, industrial problems, economic difficulties, high interest rates, and much more than the average person ever knew about before. Television has opened our eyes to life and the world around us, working at times like the preaching of the law, at other times as preparation for the preaching of the gospel.

And television hands preachers the opportunities to create sermons which will help people to make some sense out of the topsy-turvy world we live in and, through the gospel, give us hope. If one were preaching on the "last things" on the first Sunday in Advent, at least part of the sermon might be an interweaving of Ray Bradbury's *The Martian Chronicles* with the gospel. Bradbury's book is concerned with the BOMB and its ultimate threat to life in the universe. The book is over thirty years old, but, as is the case with much science fiction, it could be called prophetic. In 1981, it was shown on television as a six-hour special, mostly because of the landing of the space probes on Mars.

Bradbury, incidentally, was invited by Dr. Carl Sagan to appear with him on television as a kind of celebration of that landing on Mars. As a result of the progress made in space exploration and flight, a manned landing on Mars by 1998, as Bradbury predicted in *The Martian Chronicles,*[7] is a real possibility.

One of the reasons for incorporating the story, in its entirety, into sermons, is that many people in the average congregation will have seen the television version of it, or part of the six-hour film. The preacher would be dealing with material familiar to listeners and should already have their interest. A second reason has to do with a serious weakness in the television version of *The Martian Chronicles:* The BOMB was played down as a factor (in the book it is the major factor) in the future of life on earth and the solar system. The book speaks more directly to people who are concerned that a nuclear war would wipe out all life in this world; that's the book's prediction in the last chapter, "The Million Year Picnic." The book deals with the fear of total annihilation, a dread that has surfaced over much of the face of the earth, and it stands in sharp contrast with Luke 21:25-36, which speaks of "signs in the sun and moon and stars and upon the earth distress of nations in perplexity . . . men fainting with fear at what is coming on the world . . ." But the gospel speaks of *hope,* not total destruction of life: "And then they will see the Son of man coming in a cloud with power and great glory. Now when these things begin to take place, look up and raise your heads, because your redemption is drawing near." The gospel of God's promise that Christ will return to usher in the fulness of his Kingdom is the message that might be preached over against the fantasy-about-to-become-fact television version of *The Martian Chronicles* and the prophecy in the book that we are about to destroy the world and ourselves. The book is an exercise in reality over against the rather watered-down TV special and shows things as they could be, should a nuclear war actually come about. But the gospel of our Lord tells of God's intention for people and life on earth. His death and resurrection have not been in vain. He will return at God's appointed time and usher in the "fulness of the kingdom."

Countless classics have been made into television specials and have had tremendous impact on people. Some of them are classic because they have stood the test of time and still have something to say about life and human relationships. Others of recent vintage, like *Roots,* have also captured the attention of people and made them think — and opened the way for the preaching of the Word. Since the book was made into a television movie, "Roots" has appeared in sermon titles all over the country.

The same is true of a classic short story by Rudyard Kipling, "The Man Who Would Be King." Published over half a century before it was made into a movie, offered first in theatres, it finally was shown on television. Many of those who once read it in high school or college saw it on television and, perhaps, discovered new meaning in it. The preacher who might have read the story at one time and have seen the film version, either in a theater or on television, might use it on the Sunday of the Passion and Holy Week, interweaving the Kipling story with the gospel story in what could become an enlightening biblical story sermon.

Holocaust is another example of book-into-movie-then-television special that offers the preacher opportunity to make his sermons more narrative and more powerful proclamation of the gospel.

Other types of television programming, including the daily news programs, have utilitarian value for one's preaching ministry. Many preachers picked up on the two heroic incidents associated with the crash of the Air Florida plane into a river bridge during the afternoon

rush hour. Many found powerful Lenten sermon illustrations in this news story (the incident happened in
January, 1982). The story of the man who four times
selflessly passed the helicopter's rescue line to others,
only to sink beneath the water to his death when the
helicopter returned for him, makes the cross — though
still a mystery — more understandable. Television
connects life to the lives of the people who view it — for
better or for worse — and preachers have the opportunity to extend that connection to the gospel story that
offers God's perspective on life and death, time and
eternity.

The introduction of cable television, HBO, and
satellite reception into many communities makes a
wider variety of programming available to the people in
our parishes. Some of it is quality literature turned into
movie or television stories that might have preaching
possibilities. If the pastor is aware of what is being
televised — or shown in the movie theaters — selective
viewing is easily planned and the payoff will come in
one's preaching. The time may come when pastors will
buy home video recorders so that they might record
valuable programs they can't ordinarily see, for playback at their leisure. "Television preachers" and other
religious programming could also be taped for delayed
playback, thereby enabling the pastor to see first-hand
what is happening on Sunday morning when he is
occupied with the duties of the day. The preacher could
also study the sermons and the television preachers on
such a tape and make this at least an occasional part of
one's continuing education program in preaching. The
video recorder is a tool worth considering for one's
preaching ministry. It can make the good things offered
by television more accessible to the busy pastor.

An Exercise to Improve One's Use of Resources

Short stories, I have suggested, are valuable to

preachers searching for resources with which to enrich their sermons. They also offer the opportunity for preachers to improve their ability to tell stories and make the best possible use of stories while improving their story preaching. The preacher might begin this exercise by reading a short story that has some possibilities for incorporation into a sermon and, after reading it, retell it as concisely, yet dramatically, as possible. To do this with fidelity, it will be necessary to isolate the plot, the action and the dramatic details, the dialogue, the resolution of the encounter, and the conclusion, to decide what should be eliminated and what has to be retained so that the story will have impact. The preacher should voice it into a tape recorder, play it back, analyze it, and then voice it again. The goal would be to reduce a ten- or twelve-page (or longer) story to one or two paragraphs, sufficient to tell the story effectively.

The preacher might also take a fifty-five page chapter out of a book like the previously mentioned Antoine de St. Exupery's *Wind, Sand and Stars* (for example, "Prisoners of the Sand") and attempt to retell it in two minutes or so. This is even more difficult a task than is reducing a short story to an illustration: one must decide what to eliminate and what to retain in the retelling, while remaining true to the context and the details of the extended incident. When preachers do this, they should find themselves ready to incorporate sermon illustrations which are effectively constructed. They will have learned a skill essential to the building of the biblical story sermon.

If the preacher encounters difficulty in this exercise, it is well to reread and restudy the stories of Elie Wiesel, Fred Buechner, Fred Craddock, John Vannorsdal, and others who know how to tell stories with precision and power. By their use of language, some of these writers demonstrate how to tell the biblical story in more interesting and involving ways. Elizabeth Achtemeier singles out one among them as a model for preachers:

> *[P]erhaps Frederick Buechner is the most widely known among such preachers. Buechner's genius as a writer is the ability to recast the biblical literature into new forms of narrative and biography, sometimes successfully recapturing the original impact of the Scriptures, sometimes missing the full dimensions of their certainty, but nevertheless introducing us to a compelling homiletical model.* [8]

When we understand how Buechner and the other tellers of The Story have mastered the art of biblical storytelling, we should be on the way to mastering the art of the biblical story sermon ourselves.

There is a bonus in all of this study of story, storytellers, and The Story: the combination reveals most of the secrets of holistic preaching that complement the worship (the Song) of the people gathered for thankful and adoring response to God's actions in Christ. We learn to *rethink* and *relive* stories and The Story in apposition to each others, and this enables us to *rethink* and *retell* The Story in the pulpit with spontaneity and freshness. If telling The Story does not come together in the pulpit, in the delivery of the sermon, it won't come together at all. Except, of course, for dialogue, the storyteller does not recite stories by memory. Instead, he or she rethinks and relives them so that they come alive again as they are told. The Story — because it is a story that must be told — is a call to the conception, construction, and communication of the gospel, which can change people's lives and build up their faith in God — through a narrative sermon. Then The Story (as told by God's preachers) and the Song of God's people, in response to that Story, will be heard throughout the land.

Postscript on Collecting and Retaining Stories and Illustrations

All the preachers I know who have made extensive and effective use of secular story in their sermons have developed some kind of system for collecting and filing the sermon materials that their reading, observation, and perception have discovered. Such systems vary from the use of notebooks and journals to complicated files set up according to the Dewey Decimal System or the Library of Congress system of classifying illustrations, quotations, and stories. It is of fundamental importance that preachers have a system; that system must be personalized so that it is of maximal usefulness to the individual preacher.

Such a system ought to be simple in concept and utility. A notebook or a recipe box with 3x5 cards — or several topically indexed file folders — will do for a start. As one's perception increases, the system can be revised and expanded. An audio tape recorder is essential in this process and ought to be utilized for "making notes" on reading and observations which can be used later or even transcribed into a written record. Some pastors are already making use of video recorders, and the time will come when computers will be the tool to employ for storing sermonic materials, and perhaps word processors will play a part in sermon preparation.

It ought to be a rather compact system that is kept up to date. Otherwise, the preacher will collect all manner of items for use in preaching that will never find use. The collected materials ought to be culled out from time to time and extraneous illustrations discarded. Better yet, the preacher who is working with a long-term plan for preparing sermons, who has some idea what sermons he or she will be preaching during the coming year, and who is attuned to the church year's cycles, will be able to collect stories and other materials with selectivity. Those illustrations which are timeless and pertinent, dramatic and gripping, will be those worth retaining for future use.

Select and collect sermon materials with care. The use of copying equipment makes the task of collecting illustrations from newspapers and magazines a relatively easy one. And a usable filing system assures that the preacher will not run out of sermon-stories but will usually have the needed illustration readily available. Story sermons then become feasible as a weekly sermonic reality within the Song sung by the people of God.

180

Notes

Chapter 1

1. Mary Sharp, *A Guide to the Churches of Rome.* (Philadelphia and New York: Chilton Books, 1966), p. 69.
2. Adrian Nocent, *The Future of the Liturgy.* (New York: Herder and Herder, 1963), p. 93.
3. Clyde Reid, *The Empty Pulpit.* (New York: Harper and Row, 1967), p. 9f. "The emptiness of which I speak is an absence of meaning, a lack of relevance, a failure in communication . . . (and) there is often no message heard, no results seen, no power felt."
4. Nocent, op. cit., p. 19f.
5. Nocent, op. cit., p. 77.
6. Nocent, op. cit., pp. 42, 72.
7. Thomas Keir, *The Word in Worship.* (Nashville: Abingdon, 1962), p. 92.
8. Keir, p. 95. Nocent also comments: *"Cantare amantis est,* wrote St. Augustine. The text in the liturgy is never read . . . but it is always *proclaimed.* Time has slowly transformed this proclamation into a song." p. 116 *(The Future of the Liturgy).*
9. *Luther's Works,* vol. 35, Word and Sacrament. (Philadelphia: Muhlenberg Press, 1960), p. 358.
10. Keir, p. 94.
11. William Skudlarek, *The Word in Worship. Preaching in a Liturgical Context.* (Nashville: Abingdon, 1981), p. 9. See, also, the chapter on "Preaching and Sacrament."
12. Skudlarek, p. 9.
13. Skudlarek has a chapter on "The Bible and the Liturgical Year."
14. Nocent, p. 33.
15. James Huston, *Gig.* (New York: Dial Press, 1969), p. 28.
16. Herbert Lindemann, *The New Mood in Lutheran Worship.* (Minneapolis: Augsburg, 1971), p. 83.
17. Mandus Egge, ed., *Worship: Good News in Action.* (Minneapolis: Augsburg, 1973), p. 88.
18. William H. Willimon, *Worship as Pastoral Care,* (Nashville: Abingdon, 1979), discusses this on p. 183f.
19. Willimon, p. 21f.
20. Reid, op. cit., pp. 25-33.
21. Keir, op. cit., p. 119.
22. See *Luther's Works,* vol. 35, p. 121.
23. Sir Walter Scott, *The Heart of Midlothian.*
24. John Killinger, *The Centrality of Preaching in the Total Task of the Ministry.* (Waco, Texas: Word Books, 1969), talks about the importance of preaching; in *Experimental Preaching,* (Nashville and New York: Abingdon, 1973), makes this comment on p. 17.

Chapter 2

1. Allen Temko, *Notre Dame of Paris.* (New York: Times, Inc., 1962), p. 269.
2. Temko, op. cit., p. 295.
3. In an unpublished lecture.
4. *Luther's Works,* vol. 35, *Word and Sacrament.* (Philadelphia: Muhlenberg

Press, 1960), p. 117.

5. *Luther's Works,* vol. 35, *Prefaces to the New Testament.*

6. Loc. cit.

7. Op. cit., pp. 360-361.

8. The same unpublished lecture.

9. Richard Jensen, *Telling the Story.* (Minneapolis: Augsburg, 1980), p. 11.

10. Jensen, pp. 28-41.

11. James W. Cox, "The Impact of Worship on Preaching," p. 20f., in *Preaching and Worship,* papers published by the American Academy of Homiletics, 1980.

12. Cox, loc. cit.

13. *Liturgy: The Calendar,* vol. 1, no. 2, "The Bible and Christian Prayer," p. 5.

14. Reeder, loc. cit.

15. Gerard Sloyan, *Liturgy: The Calendar,* op. cit., "The Bible and Christian Prayer," p. 5.

16. Arndt L. Halvorson, *Authentic Preaching.* (Minneapolis: Augsburg, 1982), p. 48.

17. Andrew W. Blackwood, *Preaching from the Bible.*

18. Halvorson, p. 69f.

19. See my *The Renewal of Liturgical Preaching.* (Minneapolis: Augsburg, 1967), p. 106f.

20. Bass, "All the Saints," in *The Renewal of Liturgical Preaching,* p. 136.

Chapter 3

1. See pp. 3-7 in *The Renewal of Liturgical Preaching,* for Herman G. Stuempfle's discussion on this question.

2. Reginald Fuller, *What Is Liturgical Preaching?* (London: Student Christian Movement Press, 1957).

3. The North American Academy of Liturgics and the American Academy of Homiletics met together to discuss this relationship for the first time at Atlanta, Georgia, January, 1982.

4. *Word and Table.* (Nashville: Abingdon, 1976), p. 13.

5. David Babin, *Week-In, Week-Out. Another Look at Liturgical Preaching.* (New York: Seabury Press, 1976), p. 54f.

6. Babin, p. 61. Fred H. Lindemann said the same thing in his *The Sermon and the Propers.*

7. See Paul Bosch's *The Sermon as Part of the Liturgy.* The Preacher's Workshop Series, vol. 7 (St. Louis: Concordia Publishing House, 1977).

8. Gerard S. Sloyan, *To Hear the Word of God.* (New York: Herder and Herder, 1965), p. 13.

9. Richard R. Caemmerer, *Preaching for the Church.* (St. Louis: Concordia Publishing House, 1959), p. 1.

10. Richard Lischer, *A Theology of Preaching.* (Nashville: Abingdon, 1981), pp. 30-31.

11. Gustav Wingren, *The Living Word.* (Philadelphia: Fortress, 1958), p. 19.

12. Lischer, p. 30.

13. H. Grady Davis, *Design for Preaching.* (Philadelphia: Fortress, 1958), p. 202f.

14. Sloyan, op. cit., pp. 11-12.

15. James Armstrong, *Truth: The Foolishness of Preaching in a Real World.* (Waco, Texas: Waco Books, 1977).

16. Domenico Grasso, *Proclaiming God's Message*. (South Bend: Notre Dame Press, 1965), in which he also says that "listening to a sermon is the highest form of worship . . ."

17. Published by Concordia, 1959. Lindemann uses one introduction for the first two volumes, another for the last two.

18. Halvorson, p. 117.

19. Halvorson, p. 118.

20. Reginald Fuller, "Preparing the Homily," *Worship*, vol. 48, no. 8, 1974.

21. Fuller, "Preparing the Homily," p. 457.

22. Fuller, p. 457.

23. Antoine de Saint Exupery, *Wind, Sand and Stars*. (New York: Time, Inc., 1961).

24. Clement Welsh, *Preaching in a New Key*. (Philadelphia: United Church Press, 1974), p. 16.

25. Welsh, p. 105.

26. Charles L. Rice, *Interpretation and Imagination*. (Philadelphia: Fortress Press, 1970), p. 23.

Chapter 4

1. Elizabeth Achtemeier, "The Artful Dialogue," *Interpretation,* vol. xxxv, no. 1, (Richmond, Virginia: Union Theological Seminary, January, 1981), pp. 20-21.

2. Achtemeier, p. 21.

3. Achtemeier, p. 22.

4. Achtemeier, p. 23.

5. Achtemeier, p. 28.

6. Achtemeier, p. 29.

7. Davis, op. cit., p. 157f.

8. Clarence E. Macartney, *Preaching Without Notes*. (New York: Abingdon-Cokesbury Press, 1946), p. 9.

9. William L. Stidger, *Sermon Nuggets in Stories*. (New York: Abingdon, 1946), p. 91.

10. Stidger, p. 9.

11. My *The Renewal of Liturgical Preaching* was also published on that day, September 15, 1967.

12. John Killinger, ed., *Experimental Preaching*. (Nashville and New York: Abingdon, 1973), p. 9.

13. Bass, op. cit., p. 21.

14. McCurley is an Old Testament scholar who writes about preaching.

15. Elizabeth Achtemeier, *Creative Preaching: Finding the Words*. (Nashville: Abingdon, 1980), p. 117.

16. Richard Jensen, *Telling the Story*. (Minneapolis: Augsburg, 1981).

17. William J. Carl's response to Don M. Warlaw's "Eventful Sermon Shapes," *Preaching and Story*, Academy of Homiletics, 1979, p. 40.

Chapter 5

1. Donald Capps, *Pastoral Counseling and Preaching*. (Philadelphia: Westminster Press, 1980), p. 121f.

2. Capps, p. 125.

3. Davis, op. cit., p. 157.

4. Davis, p. 161.

5. loc. cit.

6. Edmund A. Steimle, "Preaching," *Partners,* June, 1979, p. 24. (Published by the Lutheran Church in America.)

7. Edmund A. Steimle, Morris G. Niedenthal, Charles L. Rice, *Preaching the Story.* (Philadelphia: Fortress, 1980), p. 71.

8. Steimle, Niedenthal, Rice, pp. 8-9.

9. Steimle, Niedenthal, Rice, p. 130.

10. Steimle, Niedenthal, Rice, p. 165f.

11. Steimle, Niedenthan, Rice, p. 169f.

12. Steimle, Niedenthal, Rice, p. 171f.

13. Steimle, Niedenthan, Rice, p. 173f.

14. Dan Via, *The Parables: Their Literary and Existential Dimension.* (Philadelphia: Fortress, 1967), p. 70f.

15. Via, pp. 96f.

16. John Killinger uses this same phrase in his *The Centrality of Preaching in the Total Task of the Ministry.*

17. They are to be found in *The Gift, the Glitter, and the Glory* (1981) and *The Man, the Message, and the Mission* (1983) C.S.S. Publishing Company, Inc.

18. Achtemeier, p. 106.

19. John Killinger uses this same phrase in his *The Centrality of Preaching in the Total Task of the Ministry.*

20. Edmund A. Steimle, *God the Stranger.* (Philadelphia: Fortress, 1979), p. 12.

Chapter 6

1. Steimle, in *Partners,* June, 1979, p. 24.

2. Achtemeier, op. cit., p. 106.

3. Andrew Blackwood's list.

4. Ian Macpherson, *The Art of Illustrating Sermons.* (New York, Nashville: Abingdon, 1964), p. 13f.

5. This list comes mainly from Macpherson.

6. George M. Bass, " 'A Story Told' — in Sacred and Secular Perspective," *Preaching and Story,* Academy of Homiletics, 1969, p. 63.

7. Steimle, *Partners,* p. 24.

8. Richard Thulin, "First Person Narrative Preaching," an unpublished paper given at the Academy of Homiletics, 1982, p. 3.

9. Thulin, p. 6.

10. Thulin, p. 8.

11. Thulin, p. 9.

12. Thulin, p. 11.

13. Thulin, p. 13.

14. Thulin, p. 13.

15. Nikos Kazantzakis, *Report to Greco.* (New York: Simon and Schuster, 1965), p. 101.

16. Kenneth Heuer wrote the introduction to "The Lost Nature Notebooks of Loren Eiseley," *Omni,* June, 1982, p. 88.

17. Heuer, p. 88.

18. Loc. cit.

19. Caroline Shrodes, Clifford Johnson, and James Wilson, *Reading for Rhetoric.* (New York: Macmillan Company, 1969), p. 240.

20. Loren Eiseley, *The Night Country.* (New York: Charles Scribner's Sons, 1971), p. xi.

21. Eiseley, p. 191.

22. Eiseley, pp. 170-171.

23. Eiseley, p. 171.
24. Eiseley, p. 177.
25. Eiseley, pp. 177-178.

Chapter 7

1. Mary Sharp, op. cit., p. 13.
2. Jensen, op. cit., p. 150.
3. Thor Hall, *The Future Shape of Preaching*. (Philadelphia: Fortress, 1971), p. 90.
4. Richard Lischer, op. cit., p. 25.
5. Lischer, p. 25.
6. Loc. cit.
7. Lischer, pp. 25-26.
8. George M. Bass, "Video-tape: A Prescription for Preaching." Lutheran Quarterly, 1969.
9. Andrew W. Blackwood, *The Preparation of Sermons*. (New York and Nashville: Abingdon-Cokesbury, 1948), p. 198.
10. Loc. cit.
11. Clyde Fant, *Preaching for Today*. (New York: Harper and Row, 1975), p. 112f.
12. Davis, op. cit., p. 265f.
13. Fant, p. 119.
14. Fant, pp. 119-120. Lowell Erdahl, *Preaching for the People*. (Minneapolis: Augsburg, 1972), develops a similar theory.
15. Fant, p. 122f.
16. Fant, p. 23.
17. Macartney, op. cit., p. 145.
18. Macartney, p. 144.
19. Macartney, p. 144f.
20. Macartney, p. 169.
21. Macartney, p. 170.
22. Jensen, op. cit., pp. 149-150.

Chapter 8

1. Arndt Halvorson, op. cit., p. 113.
2. Some of Weatherhead's most popular sermons are included in this collection.
3. Halvorson, p. 114.
4. Halvorson, p. 135.
5. Halvorson, p. 137.
6. Antoine de St. Exupery, *Wind, Sand and Stars*, p. 159.
7. Ray Bradbury, *The Martian Chronicles*. (New York: Time, Inc., 1963).
8. Elizabeth Achtemeier, "The Artful Dialogue," p. 28.